# How to Start a

# Youtube

# Channel

A Step by Step of Creating a great YouTube Channel, Niche Research, Target Audience, High-Quality Content, SEO, and How to Optimize Your Channel Growth and Monetization

Westin Chase

# *Table of Contents*

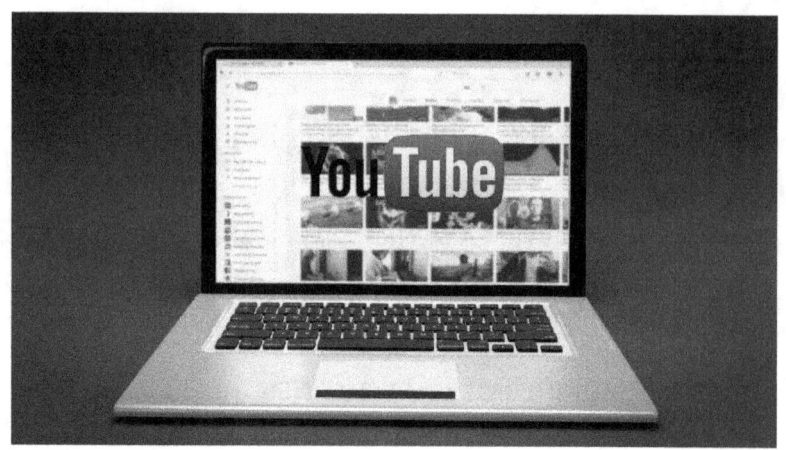

*START YOUR CHANNEL!*

*GROW YOUR CHANNEL!    AND*

*MONETIZE YOUR CHANNEL!*

# THE

# COMPLETE

# GUIDE

# INTRODUCTION

## *INTRODUCTION TO YOUTUBE CHANNEL CREATION*

In the vast digital land of today, where opportunities seem limitless, and creativity knows no bounds, there's a platform that stands as a beacon of possibility: YouTube. It's like a virtual universe where dreams are realized, talents are showcased, and stories are told with an impact that's as vast as the Great Plains. As Steve Jobs once said, "The only way to do great work is to love what you do," and on YouTube, this rings true as the songs of our ancestors.

Yet, amidst the river of content flowing through the platform every minute, there are hidden truths about YouTube that often go unnoticed.

Did y'all know that every sixty ticks of the clock, more than 500 hours of video are uploaded to YouTube? This staggering truth paints a picture of the sheer scale of creativity and expression that unfolds on this digital stage, a phenomenon that's woven into the fabric of our digital lives.

And here's a tidbit that might surprise you: YouTube pays its channel creators for their content. Yeah, you heard that right! Depending on various factors like the number of views, engagement, and advertising revenue, YouTube doles out greenbacks to its content creators, making it possible for folks like you and me to turn our passions into paychecks.

Creators typically earn revenue through advertisements displayed on their videos, with rates varying based on factors such as the viewer's location, the type of ad, and the overall engagement of the video. On average,

For every thousand views, YouTube pays its creators ranging from a few cents to several dollars, with top creators earning substantial six-figure incomes annually. So, if you're dreaming of turning your passion into a profitable venture,

YouTube might just be the golden ticket you've been searching for.

But why is YouTube so important in today's digital age? It ain't just a source of entertainment; it's a global platform where individuals can make their mark, share their passions, and carve out their own unique space in the digital landscape. From teachings to heartfelt tales, YouTube offers a canvas for self-expression and entrepreneurship unlike any other, empowering creators to reach audiences far and wide with their message.

Consider the story of Sarah, a recent college graduate with a passion for makeup but no formal training. Determined to share her love for beauty with the world, she set out on a journey to start her own YouTube channel. Armed with nothing but a smartphone and a dream, she uploaded her first video, unsure of what to expect.

To her amazement, her genuine spirit and passion resonated with viewers, propelling her to success in a matter of moons. Through dedication and perseverance, Sarah not only became an expert in her field but also monetized her channel, turning her passion into a profitable online business.

As you set out on your own journey into the world of YouTube channel creation, this book serves as your guide and companion. By the time you reach the end of these pages, you'll possess a comprehensive roadmap for starting, growing, and monetizing your own channel, no matter where your path began.

Through practical wisdom, actionable strategies, and real-life examples, you'll be empowered to turn your passion into a thriving online presence.

So, join us as we explore the boundless opportunities that await on YouTube, and remember, you ain't walking this path alone. With the right mindset and guidance, your dreams can take flight in the digital skies.

# UNDERSTANDING THE IMPORTANCE OF YOUTUBE

In today's digital age, YouTube has become more than just a platform for watching videos—it's a cultural phenomenon that has revolutionized the way we consume content, share information, and connect with others. Understanding the importance of YouTube goes beyond its entertainment value; it encompasses its profound impact on education, business, and society as a whole.

First and foremost, YouTube serves as a vast repository of knowledge and learning resources. With millions of tutorials, how-to guides, and educational videos covering virtually every topic imaginable, It has enabled people to acquire new skills and democratized access to knowledge, pursue their passions, and broaden their perspectives while remaining cozy in their own homes. From cooking recipes and DIY projects to academic lectures and language lessons,

YouTube offers a wealth of educational content that caters to diverse interests and learning styles.

Furthermore, YouTube has become a potent platform for businesses and content creators to connect and interact with their target consumers. It offers a platform for brands to highlight their goods, services, and experience, increase brand awareness, and meaningfully engage with potential clients because to its wide user base and global reach. Whether through engaging video ads, sponsored content, or influencer collaborations, businesses can leverage YouTube to drive traffic, generate leads, and ultimately increase sales.

In addition to its educational and commercial significance, YouTube plays a significant role in shaping culture and society. From viral videos and meme trends to social commentary and political discourse, it reflects and amplifies the voices, perspectives, and movements that define our times.

It has democratized media production and distribution, enabling individuals and communities to share their stories, express their creativity, and advocate for social change on a global scale.

Ultimately, the importance of YouTube lies in its ability to inform, entertain, and inspire millions of people around the world. As a platform that transcends geographical, cultural, and linguistic barriers, it has the power to educate, and empower individuals from all walks of life. By understanding and harnessing the potential of YouTube, We can take advantage of its potential to make a difference, positive impact, foster meaningful connections, and shape the future of media and communication.

## *POTENTIAL BENEFITS OF STARTING A YOUTUBE CHANNEL*

Starting a YouTube channel can offer a multitude of benefits, ranging from personal fulfilment and creative expression to professional growth and financial opportunities. Here are some potential benefits of embarking on your YouTube journey:

12

**Creative Outlet:** By starting a YouTube channel, you may let your imagination run wild and introduce the world to your own viewpoint. Whether you're passionate about cooking, gaming, beauty, or vlogging, YouTube provides a platform to express yourself and explore your interests in a creative and engaging way.

**Building a Personal Brand:** As you create and publish content on your YouTube channel, you have the opportunity to cultivate a personal brand and establish yourself as an authority in your niche.

Consistent branding, high-quality content, and engaging storytelling can help you attract and retain an audience, leading to increased visibility and recognition within your industry.

**Community Engagement:** YouTube fosters a sense of community and connection among creators and viewers alike. By engaging with your audience through comments, live streams, and social media interactions, you can build meaningful relationships, foster a loyal following, and create a supportive community around your channel.

**Monetization Potential:** While not guaranteed, Successful YouTube channels may be able to make money via a variety of monetization strategies, such as advertising, sponsorships, merchandise sales, and channel memberships. As your channel grows in popularity and reach, you can explore different avenues to make money off of your material and develop a steady source of revenue from your hobby.

**Professional Development:** Running a YouTube channel requires a diverse set of skills, including content creation, video editing, marketing, and audience engagement. By honing these skills and navigating the challenges of building and growing a channel, you can develop valuable competencies that are applicable to various professional endeavors, such as digital marketing, content creation, and entrepreneurship.

**Platform for Learning and Growth:** Launching a YouTube channel is a journey of continuous learning and growth. As you experiment with different content formats, engage with audience feedback, and adapt to changes in the YouTube landscape, you'll gain valuable insights, refine your skills, and evolve as a creator.

**Impact and Influence:** Through your YouTube channel, you have the opportunity to make a positive impact and influence others in meaningful ways.

Whether you're sharing educational content, raising awareness about important issues, or simply spreading positivity and inspiration, your voice has the power to resonate with and inspire people around the world.

Overall, starting a YouTube channel can be a rewarding and fulfilling endeavor that offers a wealth of opportunities for personal and professional growth. By leveraging your creativity, passion, and dedication, you can create content that resonates with audiences, builds communities, and leaves a lasting impact on the platform and beyond.

# *OVERVIEW OF THE STEPS INVOLVED*

Embarking on the journey of starting a YouTube channel involves several key steps, each essential for laying the foundation for success.

Here's an overview of the steps involved in launching your own channel. The full details would be discussed in the subsequent chapters:

**Define Your Niche:** Determine the focus and theme of your YouTube channel. Consider your interests, passions, and expertise, and identify a niche that aligns with your content goals and target audience.

**Research and Planning:** Conduct thorough research to understand the competitive landscape and audience preferences within your chosen niche. Identify popular content topics, keywords, and trends, and develop a content strategy and plan for your channel.

16

**Create Your Brand Identity:** Establish a cohesive brand identity for your channel, including a memorable channel name, logo, and branding elements. Ensure consistency across your channel artwork, thumbnails, and video intros for a cohesive and professional look.

**Set Up Your Channel:** Create a YouTube account if you don't already have one, and set up your channel. Customize your channel layout, add a channel description, and upload a profile picture and channel banner that reflect your brand identity.

**Equip Yourself with the Right Gear:** Invest in essential equipment and tools for creating high-quality videos. This may include a camera or smartphone with a good camera, microphone, lighting equipment, and video editing software.

**Plan and Create Content:** Develop a content calendar outlining your video topics, filming schedule, and upload frequency. Provide informative and interesting material that appeals to your target audience and aligns with your channel's niche and goals.

**Film and Edit Your Videos:** Film your videos according to your content plan, ensuring high-quality audio and video production. Edit your footage by using video editing software to enhance the visual appeal, add graphics and effects, and create a polished final product.

**Optimize for Search:** You should Optimize your videos for search engine visibility by incorporating relevant keywords, titles, descriptions, and tags. Use compelling thumbnails and titles to attract clicks and engage viewers.

**Upload and Promote:** Upload your videos to your YouTube channel, ensuring they are properly categorized and tagged. Also Promote your videos across all your social media channels, website, and email list to expand your reach and attract subscribers.

**Engage with Your Audience:** Encourage viewer participation and interaction by replying to comments, soliciting input, and urging others to like, share, and subscribe to your channel. Create a community on your channel and cultivate a rapport with your viewers.

**Analyze and Iterate:** Utilize tracking tools like as YouTube Analytics to keep an eye on the effectiveness of your videos. Examine important metrics like views, duration of viewing, and audience retention to learn more about the types of material that your audience finds engaging. Over time, use this data to hone your content strategy and raise the caliber and significance of your films.

You may position yourself for success as you start your YouTube adventure by adhering to these guidelines and maintaining your dedication to your objectives. Keep in mind that developing a successful channel requires patience, persistence, and time. As such, maintain your concentration, keep learning, and take pleasure in the process of producing and disseminating material to your audience.

We'll go further into each of these processes throughout this book, including thorough instructions, useful advice, and real-world examples to help you confidently manage the process of launching and expanding your YouTube channel. Whether you're a beginner looking to launch your first channel or an experienced creator seeking to refine your strategy and expand your reach, this book is your comprehensive roadmap to success in the world of YouTube content creation.

So stay tuned as we explore each step in depth, offering insights, strategies, and actionable advice to empower you on your journey to YouTube success.

# CHAPTER 1: FINDING YOUR NICHE

## *IDENTIFYING YOUR PASSIONS AND*

## *EXPERTISE*

Identifying your passions and expertise is the crucial first step in creating a successful YouTube channel that resonates with your audience and keeps you motivated and engaged. Here's how to discover what you're truly passionate about and where your expertise lies:

**Reflect on Your Interests:** Take some time to reflect on the activities, hobbies, and subjects that genuinely excite and inspire you. Consider the topics you love to learn about, talk about, or engage with in your free time. These interests can serve as the foundation for your YouTube channel's content.

**Assess Your Knowledge and Skill Level:** Evaluate your skills, talents, and areas of expertise. What are you naturally good at? What do you have experience in? Your expertise could stem from your education, career, hobbies, or personal experiences. Recognizing your advantages will enable you to use them to produce content that will benefit your audience.

**Explore Your Curiosities:** Don't be afraid to explore new interests and curiosities. Keep an open mind and be willing to try new things, even if they're outside your comfort zone. Your YouTube channel can be a platform for learning and growth, allowing you to share your journey of discovery with your audience.

**Consider Your Audience's Needs:** Think about who your target audience is and what they're interested in. What problems or challenges do they face? How can your passions and expertise help solve those problems or fulfill their needs? Aligning your content with your audience's interests will increase engagement and attract loyal viewers.

23

**Narrow Down Your Niche:** Once you've identified your passions and expertise, narrow down your niche to a specific topic or area of focus. Avoid being too broad or generic—instead, aim to carve out a unique space within your niche that allows you to stand out and establish yourself as an authority.

**Test Your Ideas:** Before committing to a specific niche or content format, test your ideas by creating a few trial videos or pilot episodes. Pay attention to the feedback from your audience and gauge their level of interest and engagement. Use this feedback to refine your content strategy and narrow down your niche further.

**Stay True to Yourself:** Ultimately, the key to success on YouTube is authenticity. Choose a niche that aligns with your values, interests, and personality. Your passion and enthusiasm will shine through in your content, resonate with your audience, and build trust and rapport over time.

By identifying your passions and expertise, you'll lay the groundwork for a successful YouTube channel that not only fulfills your creative aspirations but also provides value and inspiration to your audience. So take the time to explore what truly lights you up and use that passion to fuel your journey as a content creator on YouTube.

# *RESEARCHING POPULAR NICHES ON YOUTUBE*

Researching popular niches on YouTube is essential for identifying opportunities and understanding the preferences of your target audience. Here's how to conduct effective research to uncover trending and lucrative niches:

**Explore YouTube Trends:** Start by browsing through YouTube's Trending tab and exploring popular videos and channels in various categories. Pay attention to recurring themes, topics, and content formats that consistently appear in the trending section. This will give you insight into what types of content are currently resonating with viewers.

**Use Keyword Research Tools:** Utilize keyword research tools like Google Trends, YouTube Search, and use Keyword Planner to find trending search phrases and subjects related to your interests. Search for keywords that have a lot of volume and little competition because these might point to profitable niches.

**Analyze Top Channels in Your Niche:** Identify the top channels in niches that align with your interests and expertise. Study their content strategies, video formats, and audience engagement tactics. Pay attention to the types of videos that perform well in terms of views, likes, and comments, as this can give you valuable insights into what resonates with viewers.

**Browse Social Media Platforms:** Expand your research beyond YouTube by exploring popular social media platforms like Instagram, TikTok, and Pinterest. Look for trending topics, hashtags, and viral content that could inspire your own YouTube channel ideas. Social media platforms often serve as early indicators of emerging trends and popular niches.

**Survey Your Audience:** If you already have an existing audience or following on social media, consider surveying them to gather insights into their interests and preferences. Ask questions about the types of content they enjoy consuming on YouTube and what topics they would like to see more of. Their feedback can help guide your niche selection process.

**Consider Evergreen Topics:** While trending topics can provide a valuable opportunity for immediate growth, don't overlook evergreen topics that have enduring popularity and appeal. Topics like health and wellness, personal finance, and lifestyle advice tend to have consistent demand over time, making them reliable niches for content creation.

**Evaluate Monetization Potential**: As you research potential niches, consider the monetization potential of each niche. Look for niches with a large and engaged audience, as well as opportunities for revenue streams such as advertising, sponsorships, affiliate marketing, and product sales.

Finding a lucrative niche that fits with your hobbies, experience, and audience preferences will be easier if you do extensive study and keep up with the most recent opportunities and trends on YouTube. Remember to stay flexible and open to experimentation as you explore different niches and refine your content strategy over time.

Let's delve into practical ways to research popular niches on YouTube using the tools mentioned:

## YouTube Trends:

Start by visiting the YouTube Trends page (https://www.youtube.com/feed/trending) to explore the latest trending videos.

Pay attention to the topics, themes, and content formats that consistently appear in the trending section.

Take note of any patterns or recurring trends, such as viral challenges, product reviews, or educational content.

Analyze the titles, thumbnails, and descriptions of trending videos to identify common keywords and topics.

## **Google Trends:**

Visit Google Trends (https://trends.google.com) and enter relevant keywords or topics related to your interests or potential niches.

Explore the search interest over time for different keywords to identify trends and seasonal patterns.

Use the "Related queries" and "Related topics" sections to discover related keywords and topics that are trending or gaining popularity.

Compare the search interest for multiple keywords to assess their relative popularity and potential as a niche.

## YouTube Search:

Use the YouTube search bar to perform keyword research and explore popular topics within your niche.

Start typing relevant keywords or phrases related to your interests, and observe the autocomplete suggestions that appear.

Pay attention to the number of search results and the views, likes, and comments on top-ranking videos for each keyword.

Analyze the titles, thumbnails, and descriptions of top-ranking videos to identify common themes and content formats.

## Keyword Planner (Part of Google Ads):

Access Google Keyword Planner (https://ads.google.com/home/tools/keyword-planner) and sign in with your Google account.

Enter keywords related to your niche or interests and select the appropriate targeting options (e.g., location, language, search network).

Review the search volume data, competition level, and suggested bid prices for different keywords.

Use the keyword ideas and related keywords provided by Keyword Planner to identify potential niche opportunities with high search volume and low competition.

## Social Media Platforms:

Explore popular social media platforms like Instagram, TikTok, and Pinterest to discover trending topics and viral content.

Follow relevant hashtags, accounts, and trends related to your niche to stay updated on the latest trends and popular content formats.

Engage with the community by liking, commenting, and sharing content, and pay attention to the feedback and reactions from other users.

By leveraging these tools and platforms, you can gather valuable insights into popular niches on YouTube and identify lucrative opportunities for content creation. Remember to stay curious, flexible, and open-minded as you explore different niches and refine your content strategy based on audience preferences and market trends.

## *ASSESSING MARKET DEMAND AND COMPETITION*

Assessing market demand and competition is crucial for identifying viable niches and positioning your YouTube channel for success. Here are practical ways to conduct this assessment:

**Keyword Research:**

Use keyword research tools like Google Keyword Planner, SEMrush, or Ubersuggest to analyze search volume and competition for keywords related to your niche.

Look for keywords with high search volume and relatively low competition, indicating strong market demand and potential opportunities to stand out.

**YouTube Search:**

Conduct searches on YouTube using relevant keywords and phrases related to your niche.

Analyze the number of search results and the views, likes, and comments on top-ranking videos to gauge market demand and competition.

Pay attention to the quality of existing content in your niche and identify areas where you can provide unique value or fill gaps in the market.

**Competitor Analysis:**

Identify top channels and creators in your niche and analyze their content, audience engagement, and growth strategies.

Study their video topics, formats, and production quality to understand what resonates with viewers and drives success.

Assess the size and engagement level of their audience, as well as their monetization strategies and revenue potential.

**Audience Engagement:**

Monitor audience engagement metrics such as likes, comments, shares, and subscriber growth for top channels in your niche.

Pay attention to the types of content that generate the highest levels of engagement and audience interaction.

Identify common pain points, interests, and preferences among viewers, and tailor your content strategy to address their needs and interests.

**Social Media Listening:**

Monitor conversations and discussions on social media platforms, forums, and communities related to your niche.

Look for trends, topics, and issues that resonate with your target audience and indicate market demand.

Pay attention to audience feedback, questions, and concerns, and use this insight to inform your content strategy and differentiate yourself from competitors.

**Surveys and Feedback:**

Conduct surveys or polls among your target audience to gather feedback on their preferences, interests, and content preferences.

Ask questions about the types of content they enjoy watching on YouTube, their favorite channels, and what they would like to see more of.

Use this feedback to validate your niche idea, refine your content strategy, and ensure alignment with audience preferences.

By thoroughly assessing market demand and competition, you can identify lucrative niche opportunities, differentiate yourself from competitors, and position your YouTube channel for long-term success. Stay informed, adaptable, and responsive to changes in the market, and continue to refine your content strategy based on audience feedback and evolving trends.

# CHAPTER 2: PLANNING YOUR CONTENT STRATEGY

## *DEFINING YOUR TARGET AUDIENCE*

Defining your target audience is essential for creating content that resonates with viewers, attracts subscribers, and ultimately grows your YouTube channel. Here's how to define your target audience effectively:

**Demographic Information:**

Start by identifying the demographic characteristics of your ideal audience, including age, gender, location, income level, education level, and occupation.

Consider factors such as lifestyle, family status, and cultural background that may influence their interests and preferences.

Utilize tools like Google Analytics, social media insights, or market research reports to gather demographic data such as age, gender, location, and income level. You can also create surveys or polls to collect this information directly from your audience.

**Psychographic Traits:**

Dive deeper into your audience's psychographic traits, such as interests, hobbies, values, beliefs, attitudes, and personality traits.

Explore their motivations, goals, challenges, and pain points to understand what drives their behavior and decision-making.

Engage directly with your audience through social media, email newsletters, or online forums. Ask open-ended questions to uncover their interests, values, beliefs, and motivations. Pay attention to the language and tone they use in their responses to understand their personality and communication style.

## Behavioral Patterns:

Analyze your audience's behavioral patterns, including their online behavior, content consumption habits, and interaction with social media platforms.

Look for patterns in their browsing habits, search queries, and engagement with content related to your niche.

Use analytics tools provided by platforms like YouTube to analyze your audience's behavior.

Look at metrics such as watch time, view duration, and click-through rates to understand their content preferences and viewing habits. Identify patterns in their behavior to tailor your content strategy accordingly.

## Needs and Desires:

Identify the needs, desires, and aspirations of your target audience and how your content can fulfill those needs.

Determine the problems or challenges they face within your niche and how you can provide valuable solutions, insights, or entertainment.

Engage with your audience through comments, direct messages, or live Q&A sessions to understand their needs and desires. Ask probing questions to uncover the challenges they face within your niche and how you can address them through your content. Use social listening tools to monitor conversations on social media platforms related to your niche.

**Existing Audience Analysis:**

If you already have an existing audience or following on social media platforms, analyze their demographics, interests, and engagement patterns.

Use analytics tools and insights provided by social media platforms to gather data on your audience's demographics and behavior.

Use analytics tools provided by social media platforms to analyze the demographics and behavior of your existing audience. Look for trends or patterns in their engagement with your content to identify similarities or differences between your current audience and your target audience.

**Competitor Audience Analysis:**

Study the audiences of competing channels or creators within your niche to understand their demographics, interests, and preferences.

Look for commonalities and differences between your target audience and those of your competitors, and identify opportunities to differentiate your content.

**Create Audience Personas:**

Develop detailed audience personas or profiles representing different segments of your target audience.

Include demographic information, psychographic traits, behavioral patterns, needs, desires, and motivations for each persona.

When developing content, make sure it speaks to your target audience by using these personas as a point of reference.

**Feedback and Iteration:**

Constantly ask your audience for input via surveys, comments, and social media engagements.

Utilize this input to improve your comprehension of your target market and modify your content approach to better suit their requirements.

Be open to iteration and adaptation as you learn more about your audience and their evolving interests over time.

By defining your target audience with precision, You can produce information that directly appeals to their interests, addresses their needs, and fosters a deeper connection with your channel. This understanding will not only attract and retain viewers but also drive engagement, loyalty, and growth over time.

## *BRAINSTORMING CONTENT IDEAS*

Brainstorming content ideas is a creative process that involves generating and refining concepts for your YouTube channel.

Here's a step-by-step guide on how to brainstorm content ideas effectively:

## 1. Understand Your Audience

*Know Your Audience:* Use the insights gathered from defining your target audience to understand their interests, preferences, and needs.

*Identify Pain Points:* Consider the challenges or problems your audience faces within your niche and brainstorm content ideas that address these pain points.

*Analyze Popular Content:* Research trending topics and successful videos within your niche to identify content ideas that resonate with your audience.

## 2. Leverage Keyword Research

*Use Keyword Tools:* To find common search phrases and subjects within your niche, use keyword research tools such as Ubersuggest, SEMrush, and Google Keyword Planner.

*Determine Long-Tail Search Terms:* Seek for low-competition, high search volume long-tail keywords; these might provide as a source of ideas for content tailored to a certain niche.

*Explore Related Topics:* Use keyword research tools to explore related topics and subtopics that align with your audience's interests and preferences.

### 3. Tap into Your Expertise and Passions

*Draw from Your Expertise:* Identify topics or subjects that you are knowledgeable and passionate about. Your expertise and enthusiasm will shine through in your content and resonate with your audience.

*Explore Your Interests:* Brainstorm content ideas based on your personal interests, hobbies, or experiences. Authenticity and passion are key drivers of engagement on YouTube.

### 4. Be Creative and Unique

*Think Outside the Box:* Challenge yourself to think creatively and come up with unique content ideas that stand out from the crowd.

*Experiment with Formats:* Explore different content formats such as tutorials, vlogs, Q&A sessions, challenges, or storytelling to keep your content fresh and engaging.

*Put a Spin on Popular Topics:* Put your own unique spin on popular topics or trends within your niche to offer a fresh perspective to your audience.

## 5. Engage with Your Audience

*Ask for Feedback:* Encourage your audience to share their ideas, suggestions, and feedback through comments, polls, or social media platforms.

*Respond to Comments:* Engage with your audience and pay attention to the questions, comments, and suggestions they provide. Use this feedback to inspire future content ideas.

Collaborate with Your Audience: Involve your audience in the content creation process by collaborating on projects, challenges, or interactive videos.

## 6. Plan for Consistency and Variety

*Create a Content Calendar:* Plan your content in advance by creating a content calendar that outlines your ideas, themes, and publishing schedule.

Balance Consistency and Variety: Strike a balance between consistent themes or series that your audience expects and new, innovative content ideas that keep them engaged and excited.

## 7. Stay Inspired and Informed

*Stay Curious:* Stay curious and open-minded, always on the lookout for new ideas and inspiration from a variety of sources.

*Stay Informed:* Stay informed about industry trends, current events, and emerging topics within your niche to stay relevant and provide timely content to your audience.

By following these steps and fostering a creative and collaborative mindset, you'll be able to generate a wide range of content ideas that resonate with your audience and help you achieve your goals on YouTube. Remember to stay flexible and adaptable, and don't be afraid to experiment with new ideas and formats to keep your content fresh and engaging.

## CREATING A CONTENT CALENDAR

Creating a content calendar is a strategic approach to organizing and planning your content schedule for your YouTube channel.

Here is how to create a content calendar effectively:

## 1. Set Clear Goals

*Define Your Objectives:* Determine the overarching goals of your YouTube channel, such as increasing subscribers, growing viewership, or driving engagement.

Identify Key Performance Indicators (KPIs): Establish specific metrics to track your progress towards your goals, such as watch time, views, likes, comments, and subscriber growth.

## 2. Know Your Audience

*Refer to Audience Personas:* Use the audience personas you developed earlier to understand the demographics, interests, and preferences of your target audience.

*Consider Audience Preferences:* Take into account the types of content your audience enjoys and responds well to when planning your content calendar.

## 3. Brainstorm Content Ideas

*Use a Variety of Sources:* Draw inspiration from keyword research, competitor analysis, audience feedback, and your own expertise and passions.

*Consider Different Formats:* Explore various content formats such as tutorials, vlogs, reviews, interviews, challenges, or behind-the-scenes content to keep your content calendar diverse and engaging.

## 4. Plan Content Themes and Series

*Establish Content Themes:* Identify overarching themes or topics that align with your channel's niche and audience interests.

*Develop Series Concepts:* Create series or recurring segments within your content calendar to provide consistency and keep viewers coming back for more.

## 5. Determine Frequency and Timing

*Choose Your Publishing Schedule:* Decide how often you'll publish new content on your channel, whether it's daily, weekly, bi-weekly, or monthly.

*Consider Peak Times:* Use insights from YouTube analytics or social media platforms to identify the optimal times to publish your videos when your audience is most active.

## 6. Create Your Content Calendar

*Use a Calendar Tool:* Choose a digital or physical calendar tool to organize your content schedule. Popular options include Google Calendar, Trello, Asana, or a simple spreadsheet.

*Outline Your Content:* Fill in your calendar with planned content ideas, including video titles, descriptions, publishing dates, and any additional notes or resources needed for each video.

*Include Supporting Assets:* Consider including additional assets such as thumbnail images, video scripts, or collaboration details in your content calendar to streamline your production process.

## 7. Review and Adjust Regularly

*Monitor Performance:* Regularly review the performance of your videos using analytics tools to assess what's working well and what can be improved.

*Adjust as Needed:* Based on your performance metrics and audience feedback, make adjustments to your content calendar as needed to optimize your strategy and achieve your goals.

## 8. Stay Flexible and Adapt

*Be Open to Change:* Remain flexible and adaptable in your approach to content creation. Don't be afraid to pivot or experiment with new ideas based on evolving trends and audience preferences.

*Experiment and Learn*: Use your content calendar as a framework for experimentation and learning. Continuously test new formats, topics, and publishing strategies to refine your approach over time.

With these steps, you'll be able to plan and execute your content strategy effectively, keep your audience engaged, and work towards achieving your channel's goals on YouTube. Remember to stay organized, stay connected with your audience, and stay committed to delivering high-quality content consistently.

# CHAPTER 3: SETTING UP YOUR YOUTUBE CHANNEL

## *CREATING A GOOGLE ACCOUNT*

Setting up your YouTube channel starts with creating a Google account, which will serve as your login credentials for accessing YouTube and other Google services.

Here's a step-by-step guide on how to create a Google account:

### 1. Visit the Google Account Creation Page

Open your web browser and go to the Google account creation page. You can access it by typing "create Google account" into the search bar or by visiting the URL: https://accounts.google.com/signup.

## 2. Fill in Your Personal Information

You will be required to provide your personal details, such as your first and last names and preferred email address, on the account creation page. Make careful selections because this email address will also be your YouTube channel name.

Make sure your Google password is secure. Make sure it's secure and not easily guessable. Google will provide feedback on the strength of your password as you type it.

Optionally, you can add your phone number and recovery email address for added security and account recovery purposes.

## 3. Verify Your Phone Number

To help safeguard your account and make sure you can retrieve it if necessary, Google might ask you to confirm your phone number. Choose whether you would like to receive verification codes by phone call or text message by entering your phone number.

To verify your phone number, enter the verification code you get on your phone.

## 4. Agree to Google's Terms of Service and Privacy Policy

Read through Google's Terms of Service and Privacy Policy, and if you agree, check the box to indicate your acceptance.

Click on the "Next" button to proceed.

## 5. Complete the CAPTCHA Verification

Google may ask you to complete a CAPTCHA verification to confirm that you're not a robot. Follow the instructions provided to complete the CAPTCHA challenge.

## 6. Your Google Account is Created

Once you've completed all the required steps, your Google account will be created, and you'll be redirected to the Google homepage.

You can now use your Google account to access various Google services, including YouTube.

## 7. Accessing YouTube with Your Google Account

To access YouTube, Simply visit https://www.youtube.com, the YouTube homepage, and click the "Sign In" icon in the upper right corner of the screen.

You can log into YouTube by entering the email address and password linked to your Google account.

Now that your YouTube channel and Google account are connected, you can begin personalizing it, adding videos, and interacting with viewers.

You can easily register a Google account and set up your YouTube channel by following these steps. Since your visitors will see your email address, make sure it represents the tone and style of your channel.

## *CREATING YOUR YOUTUBE CHANNEL*

Creating your YouTube channel is a straightforward process that allows you to showcase your content to the world. Here's a step-by-step guide on how to create your YouTube channel:

### 1. Sign in to YouTube

Visit the YouTube website (https://www.youtube.com) in your web browser.

Click on the "Sign In" button located at the top right corner of the page.

Enter the email address and password associated with your Google account, then click "Next" to sign in.

## 2. Access YouTube Studio

Click on your profile image or initials in the upper right corner of the YouTube page after logging in.

Click the drop-down menu and choose "YouTube Studio." You'll reach the YouTube Studio dashboard by doing this.

## 3. Go to Your Channel Settings

In YouTube Studio, look for the left sidebar menu and click on "Settings."

Under the "Settings" menu, select "Channel" from the options listed.

## 4. Verify Your Account (If Required)

Depending on your account status, YouTube may require you to verify your account before creating a channel.

To validate your account, do as instructed on the screen if prompted. Entering a verification code issued to your phone number may be necessary for this.

## 5. Create Your Channel

After verifying your account (if required), locate the "Create Channel" button and click on it.

You'll be presented with options to create either a personal channel or a channel for your brand or business. Choose the option that best suits your needs.

By following these steps, you'll be able to sign in to YouTube, access YouTube Studio, navigate to your channel settings, verify your account if necessary, and create your YouTube channel. Once your channel is created, you can proceed with customizing it and uploading your content.

# CUSTOMIZING YOUR CHANNEL SETTINGS

Customizing your channel settings is a crucial step in establishing your brand identity and optimizing your YouTube presence. Here's how you can tailor your channel settings to create a professional and engaging experience for your viewers:

## 1. Accessing Channel Customization Options

Once your YouTube channel is created, you can start customizing its settings to align with your branding and content strategy.

In YouTube Studio, navigate to the left sidebar menu and click on "Settings."

Under the "Settings" menu, select "Channel" from the options listed.

## 2. Channel Description and Keywords

In the "Channel" settings, you'll find options to edit your channel description and add channel keywords.

Your channel description should provide a brief overview of your channel's content, mission, and what viewers can expect.

Channel keywords are words or phrases that describe your channel's content. These keywords help YouTube understand the nature of your channel and can improve your channel's visibility in search results.

### 3. Customizing Channel Layout and Sections

Under the "Layout" tab in Channel Settings, you can customize the layout of your channel homepage.

You can choose to display featured sections, such as "Popular uploads," "Recent uploads," or "Playlists," on your channel homepage.

You can also rearrange the order of these sections to highlight specific content or playlists.

### 4. Uploading Channel Art and Profile Picture

Click on the "Customization" tab to access options for uploading channel art and profile pictures.

Channel art is the large banner image displayed at the top of your channel homepage. It's an opportunity to showcase your brand or visually represent your channel's content.

Your profile picture is that smaller image that appears next to your channel name across YouTube. Use a clear and recognizable image that represents your channel or brand.

## 5. Adding Links and Contact Information

In the "Basic info" tab of Channel settings, you can add links to your website, social media profiles, or other relevant channels.

You can also provide contact information for business inquiries or viewer communication. This information can include an email address or business phone number.

## 6. Channel Branding Watermark (Optional)

Consider adding a branding watermark to your videos, which appears in the bottom right corner of your videos. This watermark can help increase brand visibility and encourage viewers to subscribe.

You can upload a custom image or use your channel's profile picture as the watermark.

## 7. Save Your Changes

After customizing your channel settings, be sure to click the "Save" or "Publish" button to apply your changes.

Review your channel homepage to ensure that all the customizations are displayed correctly.

By customizing your channel settings, you can create a cohesive and professional-looking channel that reflects your brand identity and content strategy. Take the time to carefully consider each customization option and how it aligns with your channel's goals and audience preferences.

# CHAPTER 4: DESIGNING YOUR CHANNEL BRANDING

## DESIGNING A CHANNEL LOGO AND BANNER

Designing a channel logo and banner is essential for establishing a strong visual identity and brand recognition on YouTube.

Here's how you can create eye-catching channel branding elements:

### 1. Channel Logo

*Keep It Simple:* Design a logo that is simple, memorable, and easily recognizable, even at smaller sizes.

Reflect Your Brand: Ensure that your logo reflects your channel's content, theme, or personality.

Use Relevant Imagery or Text: Incorporate relevant imagery, typography, or symbols that represent your brand identity.

*Optimize for Visibility:* Choose colors and fonts that stand out and are legible across various devices and screen sizes.

*Create Variations:* Design variations of your logo for different use cases, such as a square version for profile pictures and a horizontal version for video watermarks.

*Tools to Use:* You can use graphic design software like Adobe Illustrator, Canva, or online logo makers to design your logo.

## 2. Channel Banner (Channel Art)

*Showcase Your Brand:* Use your channel banner as an opportunity to showcase your brand identity, content theme, or channel personality.

*Use High-Quality Images:* Use high-resolution images or graphics that are visually appealing and relevant to your channel's content.

Incorporate Branding Elements: Include your channel logo, tagline, or social media handles to reinforce brand recognition.

*Consider Channel Sections:* Design your banner with consideration for where channel sections (e.g., videos, playlists) will overlay. Leave space for these elements to ensure they don't obscure important parts of your banner.

*Keep It Consistent:* Maintain consistency with your channel's color scheme, fonts, and overall aesthetic to create a cohesive look.

*Optimize for Different Devices:* Ensure your banner is optimized for viewing on various devices, such as desktop, mobile, and TV screens.

**Tools to Use:** You can design your channel banner using graphic design software like Adobe Photoshop, Canva, or even YouTube's built-in customization tools.

## 3. Implementing Your Branding

Once you've designed your channel logo and banner, upload them to your YouTube channel by accessing your channel settings.

Navigate to the "Customization" tab, where you can upload your channel art (banner) and profile picture (logo).

Preview how your branding elements appear on different devices to ensure they're displayed correctly.

Regularly review and update your channel branding to keep it fresh and aligned with your evolving brand identity or content focus.

By designing a compelling channel logo and banner, you can effectively communicate your brand identity, attract viewers, and create a memorable visual experience for your audience on YouTube. Take the time to craft branding elements that resonate with your audience and represent your channel's unique identity and content offering.

# CHOOSING CHANNEL COLORS AND FONTS

Selecting channel colors and fonts plays a crucial role in establishing a cohesive and visually appealing brand identity on YouTube. Here's how you can choose the right colors and fonts for your channel:

## 1. Channel Colors

*Reflect Your Brand Identity:* Choose colors that reflect the personality, theme, and values of your channel. Consider the emotions and associations different colors evoke.

*Consistency is Key:* Select a primary color palette consisting of two to four main colors that will be consistently used across your channel's branding elements, such as your logo, banner, thumbnails, and video overlays.

*Contrast and Legibility:* Make sure that, particularly in thumbnails and channel banners, there is enough contrast between the text and backdrop colors to guarantee reading.

*Consider Color Psychology:* Understand the psychological effects of colors and their impact on viewer perception. For example, blue conveys trust and professionalism, while red evokes excitement and energy.

*Test Before Finalizing:* Experiment with different color combinations and test how they appear on various devices and screen sizes to ensure they look good and are legible.

Use Color Tools: Utilize online color palette generators or design tools to explore different color combinations and find the ones that best suit your brand.

## 2. Channel Fonts

*Choose Readable Fonts:* Select fonts that are easy to read, even at smaller sizes and on different devices. Sans-serif fonts are often preferred for digital screens due to their clean and modern appearance.

*Reflect Brand Personality:* Choose fonts that align with your channel's personality and content theme. For example, a tech-focused channel might opt for sleek and futuristic fonts, while a lifestyle channel might choose more casual and playful fonts.

*Limit Font Choices:* Stick to one or two fonts for consistency throughout your channel's branding. Using too many fonts can create visual clutter and dilute your brand identity.

*Hierarchy and Emphasis:* Use different font weights, sizes, and styles (e.g., bold, italic) to create hierarchy and emphasis in your channel banners, thumbnails, and video titles.

*Balance and Contrast:* Ensure that there is a balance between your font choices and channel colors. Aim for contrast between text and background colors to improve legibility.

*Test Legibility:* Test your font choices on different backgrounds and screen sizes to ensure they remain legible under various conditions.

*Explore Font Libraries:* Utilize online font libraries and resources to discover a wide range of fonts and find the ones that best fit your brand aesthetic.

## 3. Implementation

Once you've chosen your channel colors and fonts, apply them consistently across all aspects of your channel, including your logo, banner, thumbnails, video titles, and end screens.

Regularly review and refine your color and font choices to ensure they remain aligned with your channel's evolving brand identity and content focus.

Use your chosen colors and fonts to create a cohesive and memorable visual experience that resonates with your audience and reinforces your brand identity.

By carefully selecting channel colors and fonts that reflect your brand identity and content theme, you can create a visually appealing and cohesive YouTube channel that stands out and leaves a lasting impression on your viewers. Experiment with different combinations until you find the ones that best represent your unique brand personality and resonate with your target audience.

## *CREATING A CHANNEL TRAILER*

Creating a channel trailer is an effective way to introduce new viewers to your channel and entice them to subscribe.

Here's how you can create a compelling channel trailer:

## 1. Define Your Objective

Before you start filming, determine the primary goal of your channel trailer. Do you want to showcase your best content, introduce yourself to new viewers, or encourage subscriptions? Having a clear objective will guide the content and messaging of your trailer.

## 2. Keep It Short and Engaging

Aim for a duration of around 1-2 minutes for your channel trailer. Keep it concise and attention-grabbing to maintain viewer interest throughout.

Use engaging visuals, captivating storytelling, and dynamic editing techniques to hook viewers from the start and keep them watching until the end.

## 3. Introduce Yourself and Your Channel

Start by introducing yourself and providing a brief overview of your channel's content and what viewers can expect to find.

Highlight your channel's unique selling points, such as your expertise, personality, or the value proposition of your content.

## 4. Showcase Your Best Content

Feature snippets or highlights from some of your best-performing or most representative videos to give viewers a taste of what your channel has to offer.

Select content that showcases the variety and quality of your videos while also aligning with your channel's niche and target audience.

## 5. Call to Action

Encourage viewers to subscribe to your channel at the end of your trailer. Clearly communicate the benefits of subscribing, such as receiving notifications for new uploads or gaining access to exclusive content.

You can also prompt viewers to engage with your channel by liking, commenting, or sharing the video.

## 6. Branding and Visuals

Ensure that your channel trailer reflects your brand identity and aesthetic. Use consistent branding elements such as logos, colors, and fonts throughout the video.

Incorporate visually appealing shots, graphics, and text overlays to enhance the storytelling and capture viewers' attention.

## 7. Music and Audio

Choose background music that complements the tone and style of your channel trailer. Select tracks that are upbeat, energetic, and royalty-free to avoid copyright issues.

Pay attention to audio quality and ensure that voiceovers or narration are clear and easy to understand.

## 8. Edit and Polish

Use video editing software to assemble and refine your channel trailer. Cut out any unnecessary footage, add transitions, and fine-tune the pacing to create a polished final product.

Experiment with different editing techniques, such as montages, overlays, or text animations, to make your trailer visually engaging.

## 9. Test and Iterate

Once you've created your channel trailer, preview it yourself and gather feedback from others to identify areas for improvement.

Don't be afraid to make revisions and iterate on your trailer until you're satisfied with the final result.

## 10. Upload and Promote

Upload your channel trailer to your YouTube channel and set it as the featured video on your homepage.

Share your trailer across your social media channels, website, and email newsletter to attract new viewers and encourage subscriptions.

By following these steps, you can create a compelling channel trailer that effectively showcases your channel's content, personality, and value proposition, ultimately enticing viewers to subscribe and engage with your content.

# CHAPTER 5: UNDERSTANDING YOUTUBE'S POLICIES AND GUIDELINES

## *FAMILIARIZING YOURSELF WITH YOUTUBE'S COMMUNITY GUIDELINES*

Before diving into content creation for your YouTube channel, it's essential to familiarize yourself with YouTube's Community Guidelines. These guidelines serve as the framework for acceptable behavior and content on the platform, ensuring a safe and positive experience for all users. These are the key points to keep in mind:

### 1. Respectful Behavior:

YouTube prohibits content that promotes violence, harassment, hate speech, discrimination, or threats directed towards specific people or groups because to characteristics like race, ethnicity, religion, gender identity, sexual orientation, handicap, etc.

Show respect for other people and abstain from actions that can threaten or intimidate them.

## 2. Safety:

Content that promotes dangerous activities or poses a risk of harm to viewers is not allowed. This includes but is not limited to instructional material on bomb-making, drug abuse, or self-harm.

Ensure that your content does not encourage viewers to engage in activities that could result in injury or harm.

## 3. Nudity and Sexual Content:

YouTube has strict policies regarding nudity, sexual content, and adult content. Content that contains explicit sexual material, nudity, or sexually suggestive content is not allowed.

Ensure that your content is suitable for a broad audience, including minors.

## 4. Misinformation and Harmful Content:

YouTube prohibits the spread of misinformation, deceptive practices, scams, and content that promotes harmful or dangerous activities, such as misinformation about health or medical treatments.

Verify the accuracy of information before sharing it on your channel, and avoid spreading false or misleading information.

## 5. Spam and Misleading Practices:

Avoid engaging in spammy or deceptive practices, such as artificially inflating video views, likes, comments, or subscriptions.

Provide clear and accurate information about your content, and avoid using misleading metadata, thumbnails, or titles to attract viewers.

## 6. Ad-Friendly Content:

Keep in mind YouTube's advertiser-friendly content guidelines, which outline the types of content that are eligible for monetization through ads.

Content that is considered sensitive, controversial, or not suitable for all advertisers may be demonetized or limited in ad revenue.

## 7. Reporting and Enforcement:

YouTube relies on its community to report content that violates its Community Guidelines. If you come across content that you believe violates these guidelines, you can report it to YouTube for review.

Violations of YouTube's Community Guidelines may result in various consequences, including content removal, channel strikes, or termination of your YouTube channel.

By familiarizing yourself with YouTube's Community Guidelines and adhering to them when creating and uploading content to your channel, you can ensure that your channel remains in good standing and provides a safe and positive experience for viewers.

# UNDERSTANDING COPYRIGHT AND FAIR USE

Understanding copyright and fair use is crucial for content creators on YouTube to avoid legal issues and ensure compliance with intellectual property laws. Here's a breakdown of key concepts to keep in mind:

## 1. Copyright Basics:

The exclusive rights to original works, such as films, music, photos, and other creative materials, are granted to creators under copyright law.

Once content is produced and fixed in a tangible form, copyright protection is automatically applied to it, such as recorded video or written text.

Copyright owners have the right to control how their work is used, reproduced, distributed, and publicly displayed.

## 2. Fair Use Doctrine:

A legal doctrine known as "fair use" permits, in some situations, the restricted use of content protected by copyright without the owner's consent.

The fair use doctrine takes into account a number of variables, including the use's intent and character, the kind of copyrighted work, the amount and caliber of the portion utilized, and the effect of usage on the potential market for the copyrighted work.

Criticism, commentary, news reporting, education, scholarly work, research, and satire are a few instances of fair use.

### 3. Determining Fair Use:

Determining whether the use of copyrighted material qualifies as fair use requires a case-by-case analysis, considering the specific context and purpose of the use.

There are no strict rules or formulas for determining fair use, but creators can assess their use of copyrighted material by considering the four factors outlined in copyright law.

### 4. Avoiding Copyright Infringement:

Before utilizing any copyrighted material in their videos, artists should get permission from the rights owner to avoid copyright infringement.

As an alternative, authors might utilize works released under Creative Commons or other open licenses that permit repurposing, or they can create their own original content.

When using copyrighted material, creators should strive to transform the content in some way, such as through commentary, criticism, or parody, to strengthen the argument for fair use.

## 5. YouTube's Copyright Policies:

YouTube policies can be strict in place to protect copyright holders and enforce copyright law on the platform.

Content ID is YouTube's automated copyright detection system that scans uploaded videos for copyrighted material and allows copyright owners to manage and monetize their content.

Creators whose videos are flagged for copyright infringement may receive copyright strikes, which can result in various penalties, including video removal, channel suspension, or termination.

## 6. Best Practices:

When in doubt, it's best to err on the side of caution and either make original content or obtain permission from the copyright owner.

Give proper attribution to copyright owners when using their content under fair use, and provide clear disclaimers if necessary.

Stay informed about copyright laws and YouTube's copyright policies to avoid inadvertently violating copyright.

By understanding copyright law and fair use principles, creators can navigate the complexities of intellectual property rights on YouTube and create content that respects the rights of copyright owners while expressing their creativity and engaging with their audience.

# *LEARNING ABOUT MONETIZATION POLICIES*

Learning about monetization policies is essential for YouTube content creators who aim to earn revenue from their videos. YouTube offers several monetization features, but creators must adhere to specific guidelines and policies to qualify for monetization. Here's what you need to know:

## 1. AdSense Program:

YouTube's primary monetization method is through the AdSense program, where ads are displayed on your videos, and you earn a portion of the ad revenue generated.

To participate in the AdSense program, your channel must meet certain eligibility criteria, including:

- Have at least 1,000 subscribers.
- Have accumulated 4,000 watch hours in the past 12 months.
- Comply with all YouTube's policies and guidelines.

## 2. Advertiser-Friendly Guidelines:

YouTube has specific guidelines regarding the type of content that is eligible for monetization through ads.

Content that is considered controversial, sensitive, or not suitable for all advertisers may be demonetized or limited in ad revenue.

Creators should ensure that their content complies with YouTube's advertiser-friendly guidelines to maximize monetization opportunities.

### 3. Ad Formats:

YouTube offers various ad formats that creators can monetize, including:

- Pre-roll ads: Ads that play before a video starts.
- Mid-roll ads: Ads that play during a video.
- Post-roll ads: Ads that play after a video ends.
- Overlay ads: Transparent ads that overlay the bottom part of a video.

Creators can choose which ad formats to enable on their videos, but they must adhere to YouTube's policies regarding ad placement and frequency.

## 4. Affiliate Marketing:

Affiliate marketing involves promoting products or services and earning a commission for sales or referrals made through unique affiliate links.

Creators include affiliate links in video descriptions or use tracking tools to earn commissions on purchases made by viewers.

It diversifies revenue streams alongside ad revenue and other monetization features.

Best practices include choosing relevant products, providing genuine recommendations, disclosing affiliate relationships, and tracking performance for optimization.

Affiliate marketing offers creators a way to earn revenue by recommending products or services to their audience, complementing their content, and providing an additional income stream.

## 5. Other Monetization Features:

In addition to ads, YouTube offers other monetization features for eligible creators, such as:

- Channel Memberships: Subscribers can pay a monthly fee to become channel members and gain access to perks like exclusive badges, emojis, and content.

- Super Chat and Super Stickers: Viewers can purchase Super Chats and Super Stickers during live streams to highlight their messages or show support for creators.

- Merchandise Shelf: Creators can showcase and sell their merchandise directly on their YouTube channel.

Eligibility requirements and availability of these features may vary depending on your channel's location and status.

**6. Complying with Policies:**

To maintain eligibility for monetization and avoid penalties, creators must comply with YouTube's policies, including:

- **Community Guidelines:** Ensure that your content adheres to YouTube's community guidelines regarding appropriate content and behavior.

- **Copyright Policies:** Avoid using copyrighted material without permission or proper attribution to prevent copyright claims and strikes.

- **Advertiser-Friendly Guidelines:** Create content that is suitable for advertisers and complies with YouTube's advertiser-friendly guidelines.

## 7. Monitoring and Compliance:

YouTube regularly reviews channels and videos for compliance with its monetization policies.

Creators should monitor their content and channel performance regularly, address any issues or violations promptly, and stay informed about updates to YouTube's policies and guidelines.

By understanding YouTube's monetization policies and guidelines, creators can optimize their content strategy, ensure compliance, and maximize their earning potential on the platform. Regularly reviewing and adhering to these policies will help maintain a positive relationship with YouTube and advertisers while providing valuable content to your audience.

# CHAPTER 6: CREATING HIGH-QUALITY CONTENT

## *CHOOSING THE RIGHT EQUIPMENT*

High-quality content is essential for success on YouTube, and choosing the right equipment is a crucial first step. Here's a guide to selecting the equipment you need to produce professional-looking videos:

### 1. Camera:

Choose a camera of your budget and filming needs. Options range from smartphones with high-quality cameras to DSLRs and mirrorless cameras.

Look for features such as resolution (1080p or 4K), frame rate (30fps or 60fps), image stabilization, and autofocus capabilities.

Consider factors like portability, ease of use, and compatibility with accessories like microphones and tripods.

## 2. Microphone:

Superior audio quality is equally crucial as superior visual quality. Invest in a top-notch microphone to guarantee crystal-clear audio.

Options include shotgun microphones for capturing directional audio, lapel microphones for interviews or vlogging, and USB microphones for voiceovers or narration.

Choose a microphone that suits your filming style and recording environment, whether indoors or outdoors.

## 3. Lighting:

Proper lighting is essential for achieving a professional-looking video. Invest in lighting equipment to illuminate your subject and eliminate shadows.

Consider using natural light from windows or investing in studio lights, softboxes, or LED panels for consistent and adjustable lighting.

Experiment with different lighting setups to find the most flattering and visually appealing look for your videos.

## 4. Tripod or Stabilizer:

Keep your camera steady and minimize shaky footage by using a tripod or stabilizer.

Tripods provide stability for stationary shots, while stabilizers such as gimbals or handheld rigs are ideal for capturing smooth and steady motion shots.

Choose a tripod or stabilizer that is sturdy, lightweight, and compatible with your camera setup.

## 5. Editing Software:

After filming, you'll need editing software to polish your videos and add finishing touches.

Popular editing software options include Adobe Premiere Pro, Final Cut Pro, Cap Cut, and DaVinci Resolve, as well as free options like iMovie and Shotcut.

Look for editing software that offers a user-friendly interface, a wide range of editing tools and effects, and compatibility with your computer operating system.

**6. Additional Accessories:**

Depending on your filming needs, consider investing in additional accessories such as:

External hard drives or memory cards for storing and backing up footage.

Camera lenses for achieving different focal lengths and creative effects.

Camera bags or cases for protecting your equipment while on the go.

Audio interfaces or mixers for connecting multiple microphones and achieving professional audio quality.

By choosing the right equipment for your YouTube channel, you can ensure that your videos are visually appealing, professionally produced, and engaging for your audience. Experiment with different equipment setups and techniques to find what works best for your content style and budget.

# PLANNING AND SCRIPTING YOUR

# VIDEOS

Planning and scripting videos is a critical process that lays the foundation for creating engaging and effective content on YouTube. Here's a detailed guide on how to plan and script your videos effectively:

## 1. Define Your Video's Purpose:

Before you start planning and scripting your video, it's essential to clarify its purpose and objective. Ask yourself:

- What is the main message or story I want to convey?
- What do I want my audience to learn, feel, or do after watching this video?
- How will this video align with my overall content strategy and channel goals?

## 2. Conduct Research:

Once you've defined your video's purpose, conduct thorough research on your chosen topic. This may involve:

- Gathering information from credible sources such as books, articles, studies, and reputable websites.

- Watching existing videos on similar topics to understand what has already been covered and how you can provide a unique perspective.

- Interviewing experts or individuals with relevant insights or experiences related to your topic.

**3. Outline Your Video:**

Based on your research, create an outline or storyboard for your video. Your outline should include:

The main points or topics you want to cover in your video.

The order in which you will present these points to ensure a logical flow of information.

Any visual aids, graphics, or B-roll footage you plan to include to enhance your storytelling.

**4. Identify Your Target Audience:**

Consider the demographics, interests, and preferences of your target audience when planning and scripting your video. Ask yourself:

- Who am I creating this video for?
- What are their interests, needs, and pain points?
- How can I tailor my messaging and content to resonate with my audience and provide value to them?

## 5. Write Your Script:

With your outline in hand, begin writing the script for your video. Your script should:

- Start with a strong hook or introduction to grab viewers' attention and pique their curiosity.
- Clearly articulate your main points or key messages in a conversational tone that aligns with your brand and personality.
- Include transitions, anecdotes, or examples to keep viewers engaged and reinforce your points.
- End with a clear call to action, such as subscribing to your channel, leaving a comment, or visiting your website.

## 6. Practice and Refine:

Once you've written your script, practice delivering it aloud to ensure smooth and natural delivery. Pay attention to your pacing, tone of voice, and emphasis on key points. Refine your script as needed to improve clarity, flow, and effectiveness. Consider recording yourself or rehearsing in front of a mirror to fine-tune your delivery.

## 7. Incorporate Visuals and B-Roll:

Plan how you will incorporate visuals, graphics, or B-roll footage to complement your script and enhance your storytelling. Visuals can help clarify complex concepts, illustrate examples, or add visual interest to your video. Consider using slides, animations, or on-screen text to reinforce your message and keep viewers engaged.

## 8. Optimize for SEO:

Finally, optimize your video script for search engine optimization (SEO) to improve its discoverability on YouTube and other platforms. This may involve:

- Incorporating relevant keywords and phrases naturally throughout your script.
- Writing a compelling title, description, and tags that accurately reflect the content of your video and target popular search terms.
- Considering how your video script aligns with user search intent and providing valuable content that answers viewers' questions or solves their problems.

By following these steps and investing time and effort into planning and scripting your videos, you can create compelling content that resonates with your audience, communicates your message effectively, and drives engagement and growth for your YouTube channel.

# *FILMING AND EDITING YOUR VIDEOS*

Filming and editing your videos are crucial steps in the content creation process that determine the overall quality and impact of your content. Let's explore each step in detail:

Filming Your Videos:

- Set Up Your Equipment:
- Ensure that your camera, microphone, lighting, and any additional equipment are set up correctly and in good working condition.
- Test your equipment before filming to identify any technical issues and make necessary adjustments.

**Choose the Right Location:**

- Select a filming location that aligns with the theme and content of your video.
- Consider factors such as lighting conditions, background noise, and visual aesthetics when choosing a location.
- Experiment with different angles and perspectives to find the most visually appealing shots.

**Frame Your Shots:**

- Use composition techniques such as the rule of thirds, leading lines, and framing to create visually interesting shots.

- Pay attention to the placement of subjects within the frame and the overall composition of each shot.
- Experiment with different camera angles and perspectives to add variety and depth to your footage.

## Adjust Camera Settings:

- Familiarize yourself with your camera's settings and adjust them according to the shooting environment.
- Adjust exposure, white balance, focus, and shutter speed to achieve the desired look and feel for your video.
- Use manual settings when possible to have more control over your camera's settings and achieve consistent results.

## Capture Multiple Takes:

- Record multiple takes of each scene to ensure that you have enough footage to work with during the editing process.

- Encourage natural performances from actors or participants by providing clear direction and allowing for spontaneity.
- Review each take to identify the best performances, angles, and shots before moving on to the next scene.

**Record High-Quality Audio:**

- Pay attention to audio quality, as clear and crisp sound is essential for engaging video content.
- Use external microphones or audio recorders to capture high-quality audio, and monitor audio levels throughout the filming process.
- Consider using a separate audio recorder or microphone to capture clean audio, especially in noisy environments.

**Stay Organized:**

Keep track of your footage and take notes on each shot to make the editing process smoother.

Label and organize your files systematically to avoid confusion and ensure easy access during post-production.

Create a shot list or storyboard to help guide your filming process and ensure that you capture all necessary shots.

## Editing Your Videos:

*Import Footage:*

- Transfer your footage from your camera or recording device to your computer and import it into your video editing software.
- Organize your footage into folders or bins based on scenes, takes, or other categories to streamline the editing process.

## Create a Rough Cut:

Review your footage and assemble a rough cut of your video by selecting the best takes and arranging them in the desired sequence.

Trim excess footage, adjust timing, and experiment with different pacing and transitions to create a cohesive narrative flow.

**Add Visual Enhancements:**

- Enhance your video with visual elements such as titles, graphics, overlays, and effects to reinforce your message and engage your audience.
- Use color grading, filters, and visual effects to enhance the overall look and feel of your video and create a consistent visual style.

**Enhance Audio:**

- Improve audio quality by adjusting levels, reducing background noise, and adding music or sound effects where appropriate.
- Use audio editing tools to clean up audio tracks, remove unwanted noise, and enhance clarity and intelligibility.

**Fine-Tune Your Edit:**

- Refine your edit by making subtle adjustments to pacing, timing, and visual elements to ensure a polished and professional result.

- Pay attention to details such as color correction, image stabilization, and continuity to create a seamless viewing experience for your audience.

**Review and Revise:**

- Review your video multiple times to identify any errors or areas for improvement.
- Solicit feedback from peers, collaborators, or test audiences, and be open to making revisions based on their input.
- Take breaks between editing sessions to maintain a fresh perspective and avoid fatigue-induced errors.

**Export:**

- Once you're satisfied with your edit, export your video in the appropriate format and resolution for your intended platform.
- Add metadata such as titles, descriptions, and tags to optimize your video for search and discovery.

By following these detailed steps and investing time and effort into filming and editing your videos, you can create high-quality content that captivates your audience.

## 8. Optimizing Your Videos for Search

### Conducting Keyword Research

onducting keyword research is a crucial step in optimizing your video for search engines and maximizing its discoverability on platforms like YouTube. Here's how to conduct essential keyword research for your video:

*1. Understand Your Audience and Content:*

Before diving into keyword research, it's important to have a clear understanding of your target audience and the content of your video. Ask yourself:

- Who is my target audience, and what are their interests, needs, and preferences?
- What topics or themes does my video cover, and what questions or problems does it address?
- What keywords or phrases are likely to be used by my audience when searching for content like mine?

## 2. Brainstorm Seed Keywords:

Start by brainstorming a list of seed keywords or topics that are relevant to your video content. These can be broad terms or phrases that capture the main themes or subjects of your video. For example, if your video is about "healthy breakfast recipes," your seed keywords might include "breakfast ideas," "healthy meals," and "easy recipes."

## 3. Use Keyword Research Tools:

Utilize keyword research tools to expand your list of seed keywords and identify potential keywords with high search volume and low competition. Popular keyword research tools include:

- Google Keyword Planner
- SEMrush
- Ahrefs
- Ubersuggest
- KeywordTool.io

## *4. Analyze Search Volume and Competition:*

Evaluate the search volume and competition for each keyword using your chosen keyword research tool. Look for keywords with a high search volume and relatively low competition, as these are more likely to attract traffic to your video. Additionally, consider long-tail keywords, which are longer and more specific phrases that may have less competition but can still attract targeted traffic.

## *5. Consider User Intent:*

Think about the intent behind the keywords you're targeting and how they align with the content of your video. Are users searching for informational content, product reviews, tutorials, or how-to guides? Tailor your keyword selection to match the intent of your target audience and provide valuable content that meets their needs.

## *6. Explore Related Keywords and Topics:*

Expand your keyword list by exploring related keywords and topics suggested by your keyword research tool. Look for variations, synonyms, and related terms that users might use when searching for content similar to yours. Incorporate these keywords into your video title, description, tags, and script to improve your video's visibility and relevance.

## 7. Prioritize and Refine Your Keywords:

Once you've compiled a list of potential keywords, prioritize them based on their relevance, search volume, and competition level. Focus on targeting a mix of high-impact keywords with broad appeal and long-tail keywords with specific relevance to your video content. Refine your keyword strategy based on ongoing performance analysis and feedback from your audience.

## 8. Implement Keywords Strategically:

Integrate your selected keywords strategically throughout your video metadata, including the title, description, tags, and transcript. Ensure that your keywords are used naturally and contextually within your content to improve search visibility and user engagement. Monitor your video's performance and make adjustments to your keyword strategy as needed to optimize for search and maximize exposure.

More of it will be discussed in the next sub headings.

# *OPTIMIZING TITLES, DESCRIPTIONS, AND TAGS*

Optimizing titles, descriptions, and tags is essential for improving the visibility and discoverability of your videos on platforms like YouTube. Here's how to optimize each element effectively:

## 1. Optimizing Titles:

*Include Target Keywords:* Incorporate your primary target keyword or key phrase at the beginning of your title to improve search visibility. Make sure the title accurately reflects the content of your video and entices viewers to click.

*Keep It Concise and Descriptive:* Aim for titles that are clear, concise, and descriptive. Avoid unnecessary words or filler phrases, and focus on capturing the essence of your video in a compelling way.

*Use Engaging Language:* Use action words, questions, or intriguing statements to grab viewers' attention and encourage them to watch your video. Consider incorporating emotional triggers or curiosity-inducing phrases to pique interest.

## 2. Optimizing Descriptions:

*Include Keywords Naturally:* Write a detailed and informative description that includes your target keywords in a natural and contextually relevant manner. Provide a summary of your video's content, key points, and any additional relevant information.

*Add Timestamps and Links:* Timestamps can help viewers navigate to specific sections of your video, while links to related content, resources, or your website can encourage engagement and drive traffic.

*Use Formatting for Readability:* Break up your description into paragraphs and use bullet points or numbered lists to make it easier to read and digest. Include relevant hashtags to expand your video's reach and visibility on social media platforms.

**3. Optimizing Tags:**

*Include Relevant Keywords:* Choose relevant tags that accurately describe the content and topics covered in your video. Use a mix of broad keywords and long-tail keywords to maximize your video's visibility in search results.

*Prioritize Primary Keywords:* Place your primary target keywords or phrases at the beginning of your tag list to give them more weight. Include variations, synonyms, and related terms to capture a broader range of search queries.

*Use YouTube's Auto-Suggest Feature:* Take advantage of YouTube's auto-suggest feature to discover additional relevant tags and expand your tag list. Start typing relevant keywords into the tag field and select from the suggested *options that appear.*

*Avoid Overloading Tags:* While it's important to include relevant tags, avoid overloading your video with too many tags. Focus on quality over quantity and choose tags that are directly relevant to your video's content.

By optimizing titles, descriptions, and tags with relevant keywords, engaging language, and strategic formatting, you can increase your video's visibility, attract more viewers, and ultimately grow your audience and channel on platforms like YouTube.

## Utilizing Thumbnails Effectively

Utilizing thumbnails effectively is crucial for attracting viewers' attention and encouraging them to click on your videos. Here's how to optimize your thumbnails for maximum impact:

## 1. Choose Compelling Images:

Select visually appealing images or screenshots from your video that accurately represent its content.

Use high-quality images with clear, vibrant colors and sharp details to grab viewers' attention.

## 2. Highlight Key Elements:

Emphasize key elements of your video, such as faces, text, or important objects, to convey the video's topic or message at a glance.

Ensure that the focal point of your thumbnail is easily recognizable and relevant to the video's content.

## 3. Use Text Wisely:

Incorporate concise and impactful text overlays that complement the visual elements of your thumbnail.

Use bold, easy-to-read fonts and keep text to a minimum to avoid cluttering the thumbnail.

## 4. Maintain Branding Consistency:

Maintain consistency in your thumbnail design to reinforce your channel's branding and identity.

Use consistent colors, fonts, and styles across your thumbnails to create a cohesive and recognizable visual aesthetic.

## 5. Test Different Designs:

Experiment with different thumbnail designs, images, and text overlays to see what resonates best with your audience.

A/B test different thumbnail variations to determine which ones generate the highest click-through rates.

## 6. Optimize for Visibility:

Ensure that your thumbnails are easily visible and recognizable on various devices and screen sizes.

Use contrasting colors, bold text, and clear imagery to make your thumbnails stand out in search results and suggested videos.

## 7. Follow YouTube's Guidelines:

Adhere to YouTube's thumbnail guidelines, which specify dimensions, file formats, and content restrictions.

Avoid misleading or clickbait thumbnails that misrepresent the content of your video, as this can harm your channel's reputation and credibility.

## 8. Analyze Performance:

Monitor the performance of your thumbnails using YouTube Analytics and other tracking tools.

Pay attention to metrics such as click-through rate (CTR) and impressions to gauge the effectiveness of your thumbnail designs.

Use this data to iterate and refine your thumbnail strategy over time, focusing on designs that drive the highest engagement and viewership.

By following these tips and best practices, you can create thumbnails that effectively capture viewers' attention, convey the essence of your videos, and drive higher click-through rates on platforms like YouTube.

## 9. Building Your Audience

### Engaging with Your Viewers

Engaging with your viewers is essential for building a loyal and active community around your YouTube channel. By fostering meaningful interactions and connections with your

111

audience, you can increase viewer engagement, encourage repeat visits, and cultivate a sense of belonging and loyalty. Here's how to effectively engage with your viewers:

## 1. Respond to Comments:

Regularly monitor and respond to comments on your videos to show appreciation for viewer feedback and encourage ongoing conversation.

Take the time to address questions, provide additional information, and engage in meaningful discussions with your audience.

Personalize your responses and acknowledge individual viewers by name whenever possible to make them feel valued and appreciated.

## 2. Encourage Community Interaction:

Foster a sense of community among your viewers by encouraging them to interact with each other in the comments section.

Pose questions, prompts, or discussion topics related to your video content to stimulate conversation and engagement.

Highlight and showcase insightful or positive comments from your audience to encourage further participation and collaboration.

*3. Utilize Community Features:*

Take advantage of YouTube's community features, such as polls, community posts, and live chats, to engage with your audience in real-time.

Poll your viewers to gather feedback, opinions, or preferences on upcoming content ideas, video topics, or channel updates.

Use community posts to share behind-the-scenes content, updates, announcements, or exclusive offers with your audience.

*4. Host Live Streams and Q&A Sessions:*

Host live streams or Q&A sessions to interact with your audience in real-time and answer their questions or address their concerns.

Use live chat features to engage with viewers directly, respond to their comments and questions, and create a sense of immediacy and intimacy.

Schedule regular live streams or interactive events to keep your audience engaged and connected with your channel.

*5. Collaborate with Your Audience:*

Involve your audience in the content creation process by soliciting their input, ideas, or suggestions for future videos.

Collaborate with your audience on collaborative projects, challenges, or contests to foster a sense of ownership and participation.

Showcase user-generated content or fan submissions in your videos to recognize and celebrate your audience's contributions.

*6. Be Authentic and Genuine:*

Show authenticity, transparency, and sincerity in your interactions with your audience to build trust and rapport.

Share personal anecdotes, experiences, or insights to connect with your audience on a deeper level and humanize your brand.

Be genuine in your responses and avoid scripted or robotic interactions to maintain authenticity and credibility.

*7. Analyze Audience Feedback:*

Pay attention to audience feedback, suggestions, and preferences to tailor your content and engagement strategies to meet their needs and interests.

Use analytics tools and metrics to track viewer engagement, sentiment, and behavior, and adjust your approach accordingly.

Continuously iterate and improve your engagement efforts based on audience feedback and performance data to maximize impact and effectiveness.

By actively engaging with your viewers, fostering community interaction, and soliciting feedback and input, you can cultivate a loyal and dedicated audience base that is actively invested in your content and brand. Prioritize building genuine connections and fostering meaningful interactions to create a thriving and engaged community around your YouTube channel.

# *PROMOTING YOUR VIDEOS ON SOCIAL MEDIA*

Promoting your videos on social media is a powerful way to expand your reach, attract new viewers, and drive traffic to your YouTube channel. Here's a comprehensive guide on how to effectively promote your videos on social media platforms:

## *1. Choose the Right Platforms:*

- Identify the social media platforms where your target audience is most active and engaged.
- Focus your efforts on platforms such as Facebook, Twitter, Instagram, LinkedIn, TikTok, Pinterest, or Reddit, depending on your niche and audience demographics.

## 2. Create Compelling Teasers:

- Create short, attention-grabbing teasers or trailers for your videos to share on social media.
- Use captivating visuals, intriguing captions, and snippets of your video content to pique curiosity and encourage clicks.

## 3. Optimize Your Posts:

- Craft compelling headlines, descriptions, and calls-to-action (CTAs) that entice viewers to watch your video.
- Use relevant hashtags and keywords to increase the visibility of your posts and attract users searching for related content.

## 4. Share Behind-the-Scenes Content:

- Share behind-the-scenes content, sneak peeks, or bloopers from your video production process to give your audience a glimpse into your creative process and personality.
- Humanize your brand and foster a sense of connection and authenticity with your audience.

117

## 5. Leverage Stories and Live Streams:

- Use Instagram Stories, Facebook Stories, or Snapchat to share short, ephemeral updates and highlights from your videos.

- Host live streams or Q&A sessions on platforms like Instagram Live, Facebook Live, or YouTube Live to engage with your audience in real-time and promote your latest videos.

## 6. Collaborate with Influencers:

- Partner with influencers or content creators in your niche to promote your videos to their followers.

- Collaborate on co-created content, shout-outs, or guest appearances to leverage their audience and expand your reach.

## 7. Engage with Your Audience:

- Respond to comments, messages, and mentions from your followers to build relationships and foster community engagement.

- Encourage user-generated content, such as fan art, reactions, or challenges related to your videos, and share it on your social media channels.

## *8. Schedule Posts for Optimal Timing:*

- Schedule your social media posts for times when your audience is most active and likely to engage with your content.
- Use social media management tools like Buffer, Hootsuite, or Sprout Social to plan and schedule your posts in advance.

## *9. Cross-Promote Across Platforms:*

- Share your YouTube videos across multiple social media platforms to reach a wider audience.
- Customize your messaging and content for each platform to optimize engagement and resonate with specific audience demographics.

## *10. Analyze and Iterate:*

- Monitor the performance of your social media posts using analytics tools provided by each platform.

- Track metrics such as reach, engagement, clicks, and conversions to assess the effectiveness of your promotion efforts.

- Use insights from analytics to refine your social media strategy, experiment with different tactics, and optimize your promotion campaigns over time.

By following these strategies and best practices, you can effectively promote your YouTube videos on social media, expand your audience, and increase engagement with your content. Remember to be consistent, authentic, and creative in your approach, and prioritize building genuine connections with your audience across all social media platforms.

# *COLLABORATING WITH OTHER YOUTUBERS*

Collaborating with other YouTubers is a fantastic way to expand your audience, create engaging content, and build relationships within the YouTube community. Here's a comprehensive guide on how to effectively collaborate with other YouTubers:

## 1. Identify Potential Collaborators:

Research and identify YouTubers in your niche or related niches who share a similar audience demographic and content style.

Look for creators with a comparable subscriber count, engagement level, and content quality to ensure a mutually beneficial collaboration.

## 2. Reach Out and Establish Contact:

Reach out to potential collaborators via email, direct message on social media, or through YouTube's messaging system.

Introduce yourself, explain why you're interested in collaborating, and highlight how your audiences and content complement each other.

## 3. Brainstorm Collaboration Ideas:

Brainstorm creative collaboration ideas that align with both yours and your collaborator's content and audience interests.

Consider collaborative video formats such as challenges, Q&A sessions, interviews, co-hosted videos, or themed series.

## 4. Plan and Coordinate:

Coordinate with your collaborator to plan the details of the collaboration, including video concept, filming schedule, and logistics.

Establish clear roles and responsibilities for each participant to ensure a smooth and organized collaboration process.

## 5. Promote the Collaboration:

Promote the collaboration across your respective social media channels and platforms to generate excitement and anticipation among your audiences.

Create teaser trailers, behind-the-scenes content, or countdown posts to build hype and anticipation leading up to the collaboration release.

*6. Film and Edit the Collaboration:*

Collaborate with your partner to film and produce the collaborative video, ensuring that both creators' styles and personalities are showcased effectively.

Edit the video collaboratively or delegate editing tasks to one creator, maintaining a cohesive and seamless flow throughout the video.

*7. Cross-Promote Each Other's Channels:*

- Cross-promote each other's channels and content within the collaborative video by including verbal shout-outs, on-screen graphics, or clickable links in the video description.

- Encourage viewers to subscribe to each other's channels and engage with both creators' content to foster ongoing collaboration and support.

*8. Engage with Your Audiences:*

- Engage with your audiences by responding to comments, questions, and feedback on the collaborative video.

- Encourage viewers to leave comments, share their thoughts, and interact with both creators' communities to maximize engagement and interaction.

9. Evaluate and Reflect:

Reflect on the collaboration experience and assess its impact on both creators' channels, audiences, and overall growth.

Identify lessons learned, successes, and areas for improvement to inform future collaboration opportunities and strategies.

**10. Explore Ongoing Collaboration Opportunities:**

Explore ongoing collaboration opportunities with your partner, such as co-hosting series, joint projects, or recurring collaborations to maintain momentum and foster a long-term partnership.

By following these steps and best practices, you can effectively collaborate with other YouTubers to create engaging content, expand your audience, and strengthen your presence within the YouTube community. Remember to approach collaborations with authenticity, professionalism, and a spirit of collaboration to maximize the benefits for both creators involved.

# CHAPTER 7: GROWING YOUR CHANNEL

## *ANALYZING YOUR YOUTUBE ANALYTICS*

Analyzing your YouTube analytics is crucial for understanding your channel's performance, identifying areas for improvement, and making informed decisions to optimize your content strategy.

Here's a comprehensive guide on how to effectively analyze your YouTube analytics:

**1. Accessing Your Analytics:**

Navigate to your YouTube Studio dashboard and select the "Analytics" tab to access your channel's analytics dashboard.

Explore the various sections and metrics available, including overview, reach, engagement, audience, and revenue, to gain insights into different aspects of your channel's performance.

## 2. Understanding Key Metrics:

Familiarize yourself with key metrics such as views, watch time, audience retention, likes, comments, and subscriber growth to gauge the overall health and performance of your channel.

Pay attention to metrics like average view duration, click-through rate (CTR), and audience retention graphs to assess the effectiveness of your content in capturing and retaining viewers' attention.

## 3. Analyzing Audience Demographics:

Explore audience demographics data, including age, gender, location, and device type, to understand the characteristics and preferences of your viewers.

Use demographic insights to tailor your content, messaging, and promotional efforts to better resonate with your target audience.

## 4. Tracking Video Performance:

Analyze the performance of individual videos using metrics such as views, watch time, likes, and comments to identify top-performing content and trends.

Compare the performance of different videos to uncover patterns, themes, or topics that resonate most with your audience and inform future content decisions.

## 5. Assessing Traffic Sources:

Review traffic sources data to understand how viewers are discovering your videos, whether through YouTube search, suggested videos, external sources, or direct traffic.

Identify which traffic sources drive the most views and engagement to optimize your video promotion and distribution strategies accordingly.

## 6. Monitoring Audience Engagement:

Monitor audience engagement metrics such as likes, comments, shares, and subscriber growth to gauge viewer interaction and feedback.

Respond to comments, questions, and feedback from your audience to foster community engagement and build stronger relationships with your viewers.

## 7. Setting Goals and Benchmarks:

Set specific goals and benchmarks for your channel's growth and performance based on key metrics and objectives.

Track your progress over time and adjust your strategies and tactics as needed to achieve your goals and drive continuous improvement.

## 8. Experimenting and Iterating:

Experiment with different content formats, topics, styles, and promotional strategies to test what resonates best with your audience.

Use insights from your analytics to iterate and refine your content strategy, production quality, and distribution tactics to maximize engagement and viewership.

## 9. Staying Informed with Updates:

Stay informed about updates, changes, and new features in YouTube analytics to leverage the latest tools and insights for optimizing your channel.

Follow YouTube's Creator Insider channel and blog for announcements, tips, and best practices on using analytics effectively.

## 10. Seeking Additional Resources:

Explore additional resources, tutorials, and courses on YouTube analytics and channel optimization to deepen your understanding and skills.

Join online communities, forums, or networking groups with fellow creators to share insights, ask questions, and learn from each other's experiences.

By regularly analyzing your YouTube analytics, setting goals, experimenting with content, and staying informed with updates, you can gain valuable insights into your channel's performance and drive continuous improvement to achieve your growth and engagement objectives.

# CONSISTENTLY IMPROVING AND EVOLVING YOUR CHANNEL

Consistently improving and evolving your YouTube channel is essential for staying relevant, engaging your audience, and achieving long-term success. Here's a comprehensive guide on how to effectively improve and evolve your channel over time:

## 1. Set Clear Goals and Objectives:

- Define clear goals and objectives for your YouTube channel, such as increasing subscribers, improving engagement, or expanding your reach.
- Establish specific, measurable, achievable, relevant, and time-bound (SMART) goals to guide your improvement efforts.

## 2. Conduct Regular Audits:

- Conduct regular audits of your channel's performance, content quality, branding, and audience engagement.

- Use YouTube analytics, audience feedback, and industry benchmarks to assess your channel's strengths, weaknesses, opportunities, and threats (SWOT analysis).

## 3. Identify Areas for Improvement:

- Identify areas for improvement based on your audit findings, focusing on content quality, audience engagement, channel growth, and branding consistency.
- Prioritize improvements based on their impact on your channel's goals and objectives.

## 4. Invest in Content Quality:

- Prioritize content quality by investing in equipment, software, and resources to improve production value, visual appeal, and storytelling.
- Focus on creating valuable, relevant, and engaging content that resonates with your audience and keeps them coming back for more.

## 5. Experiment with New Formats and Topics:

- Experiment with new content formats, topics, and styles to keep your channel fresh, diverse, and engaging.
- Stay abreast of trends, audience interests, and industry developments to identify new content opportunities and capitalize on emerging trends.

## 6. Engage with Your Audience:

- Foster meaningful interactions and engagement with your audience by responding to comments, messages, and feedback.
- Encourage dialogue, collaboration, and community participation to build a loyal and dedicated fan base.

## 7. Collaborate with Other Creators:

- Collaborate with other YouTubers, influencers, and content creators to expand your reach, tap into new audiences, and create compelling content.
- Leverage cross-promotion opportunities, co-created content, and joint projects to amplify your channel's impact and visibility.

## 8. Optimize Your Channel and Content:

- Continuously optimize your channel and content for searchability, discoverability, and user experience.
- Use keyword research, metadata optimization, and best practices for titles, descriptions, tags, and thumbnails to improve your video's visibility and ranking in search results.

## 9. Stay Informed and Educated:

- Stay informed about YouTube's latest features, policies, and best practices by following official announcements, blogs, and creator resources.
- Invest in ongoing learning and education to enhance your skills, knowledge, and expertise in content creation, audience engagement, and channel management.

## 10. Adapt to Feedback and Data:

- Listen to feedback from your audience and use data-driven insights from analytics to guide your decision-making and content strategy.

- Be open to constructive criticism, iterate on your content based on audience preferences, and continuously refine your approach to better meet the needs and interests of your viewers.

By consistently improving and evolving your YouTube channel, you can stay ahead of the curve, delight your audience, and achieve sustainable growth and success in the competitive world of online video content creation. Embrace a mindset of continuous improvement, experimentation, and adaptation to keep your channel thriving in the ever-changing digital landscape.

# CHAPTER 8: MONETIZING YOUR CHANNEL

If you're aiming to earn from your content creation efforts, a valuable step is mastering the art of monetizing your YouTube channel. The dependable YouTube Partner Program, coupled with its integrated advertising platform, offers a pathway to start earning revenue on YouTube with relative swiftness.

Although it's essential to maintain realistic expectations and understand that significant wealth won't materialize overnight, the accumulation of modest earnings can prove substantial over time. Additionally, as your audience grows in size and engagement, the potential financial rewards become increasingly promising.

# *HOW TO MONETIZE YOUTUBE CHANNEL*

The primary avenue for generating income on YouTube is through enrollment in the YouTube Partner Program, which facilitates monetization through advertisements and other avenues.

To qualify for the YouTube Partner Program, you must meet specific criteria:

- Maintain a channel with a minimum of 500 subscribers.

- Accumulate 3,000 valid public watch hours within the past 12 months, including YouTube Live videos, or achieve 3 million views on YouTube Shorts within the past 90 days.

- Upload at least three public videos within the last 90 days.

- Have an active AdSense account linked to your YouTube channel.

- Ensure your channel has no active Community Guidelines strikes.

- Adhere to all of YouTube's monetization policies.

- Enable two-step verification for the Google account associated with your YouTube channel to enhance online security.

While you may need to invest in equipment and other essentials, there's no upfront cost to start earning money on YouTube.

Although the platform does deduct a portion of your earnings, there are no initial fees involved.

Once you've met all the criteria for the YouTube Partner Program, it's time to initiate the process in YouTube Studio. Let's delve into the steps to activate monetization and embark on your journey to earning money on YouTube.

# HOW TO ACTIVATE YOUTUBE STUDIO

# MONETIZATION

To initiate the monetization process for your YouTube channel, follow these steps:

- Go to the YouTube homepage and click on your profile icon. From the dropdown menu, select 'YouTube Studio.'

- In the left navigation bar of YouTube Studio, locate and click on 'Monetization.'

- Once you've fulfilled the requirements, you'll notice a blue button labeled 'APPLY NOW.' Click on it to proceed. If you haven't met the criteria yet, you can opt to receive a notification when you become eligible by clicking on the 'Notify me when I'm eligible' button.

- YouTube will conduct a review to ensure compliance with their Community Guidelines. Familiarize yourself with these guidelines to avoid inadvertently violating them in the future.

- Verify that your channel's location settings are accurate to prevent any potential issues.

- Link your YouTube channel to your AdSense account. If you don't have one, you can create it at this stage. If you already have an AdSense account, simply sign in and connect it to your YouTube channel.

- Submit your application. Be prepared to exercise patience as the approval process typically takes around a month. In some cases, it may take longer as each application is manually reviewed by a human reviewer, not an automated system.

Keep in mind that while having 500 subscribers qualifies you for the YouTube Partner Program, you'll need to reach 1,000 subscribers to activate ad revenue and access YouTube Premium benefits.

Once you've activated monetization through the YouTube Partner Program and surpassed 1,000 subscribers, you gain the ability to enable ads on your videos. You can choose to monetize every video or select specific ones.

It's essential to understand that advertising revenue is influenced by various factors, not just the number of viewers. Factors such as viewer demographics, location, and engagement with your content play significant roles. Advertisers value engaged audiences, so viewers who interact with your content are more valuable than those who simply watch without engaging.

Additionally, it's crucial to use music legally and safely on the platform. YouTubers must have the appropriate rights to include music in their content. Failure to do so can result in copyright infringement issues, where the rights holder, such as the songwriter, artist, or record label, may claim ownership of the content. This mistake can lead to others monetizing your content instead of you, so it's essential to be mindful of copyright laws and obtain proper permissions when using copyrighted material.

Dealing with music copyright can indeed be a hassle. However, there's a solution: Epidemic Sound. With Epidemic Sound, you can access a vast catalog of over 40,000 tracks, all with the proper rights cleared. Say goodbye to worrying about copyright issues and start soundtracking your content safely today.

As for how much you can earn after monetizing your channel, it's a variable figure influenced by several factors:

- **Your niche:** Some niches command higher advertising rates than others, depending on advertiser demand.

- **Click-through rate:** The number of clicks your ads receive affects your earnings, as advertisers pay based on ad engagement.

- **Video length:** Longer videos generally have more opportunities for ad placements, potentially increasing your revenue.

- **Viewer demographics:** Ad rates can vary depending on where your viewers are located globally, with some regions commanding higher ad rates than others.

- **View count:** The number of views your videos receive directly impacts your earnings, as more views typically translate to higher ad revenue.

Keep in mind that these factors interact in complex ways, and there's no one-size-fits-all answer to how much you can earn. However, by creating high-quality content, engaging with your audience, and optimizing your monetization strategies, you can maximize your earning potential on YouTube.

The average pay rate on YouTube typically ranges from $0.10 to $0.30 for each ad view. YouTube retains 45% of the AdSense earnings, leaving creators with 55% of the revenue.

For established YouTubers, earnings can amount to around $18 per 1,000 ad views, translating to approximately $3 to $5 per 1,000 video views. However, a more realistic expectation is to earn between $1 to $2 per 1,000 video views.

To put this into perspective, generating over one million views per month is necessary to replace a full-time income. Consequently, many creators diversify their revenue streams beyond relying solely on Google AdSense monetization.

It's worth noting that revenue can also be generated from video views by YouTube Premium users, as YouTube shares a portion of its subscription revenue with creators. Similar to ad-generated income, YouTube takes a 45% cut of a creator's Premium earnings.

For a more detailed assessment of your earnings per 1,000 views, you can consult YouTube Analytics and review your RPM (Revenue Per Mille). RPM calculates earnings based on various factors, including ad revenue, channel memberships, YouTube Premium revenue, Super Chat, and Super Stickers. Additionally, it considers views on videos that haven't been monetized yet.

RPM, or Revenue Per Mille, differs from CPM, which stands for 'Cost Per Mille.' CPM represents the cost per 1,000 ad impressions and encompasses revenue from YouTube Premium and ads. It specifically accounts for views from monetized videos. Unlike RPM, CPM reflects the total amount before YouTube takes its cut, providing a pre-cut estimate of revenue.

**To increase your RPM, consider the following strategies:**

- Enable monetization for all videos to maximize revenue potential.
- Activate all available ad formats to capture diverse advertising opportunities.

- Place ads at all eligible positions, such as midrolls, to optimize ad placement and viewer engagement.
- Explore additional revenue streams by leveraging features like channel memberships and Super Chat.

By implementing these tactics, you can enhance your RPM and effectively boost your earnings on YouTube.

# *OTHER 6 WAYS TO MAKE MONEY ON YOUTUBE*

Many content creators monetize their YouTube channels as part of a broader strategy to generate income, with YouTube's Partner Program being just one avenue. Let's explore some monetization methods directly tied to the YouTube Partner Program, as well as other avenues:

### **Super Chat, Super Stickers, and Super Thanks**

These features allow viewers to express appreciation and support while creators earn money.

With Super Chat, viewers can donate between $1 and $500 during YouTube Live videos and premieres. Their comments are highlighted in the live chat as a reward.

Super Stickers function similarly to Super Chat, offering viewers the chance to purchase fun stickers that appear prominently in the live chat, increasing their visibility to the creator.

Super Thanks allows viewers to demonstrate gratitude by purchasing and sending a special comment accompanied by a GIF. Unlike Super Chat, Super Thanks can be used on any uploaded video, not just live streams.

Creators receive a 70% share of the revenue generated from these features, with YouTube retaining the remaining 30%. It's an engaging way for creators to interact with their audience while earning additional income.

### 1. <u>Sell your merchandise</u>

Harness the power of your content by transforming funny characters, catchy phrases, or niche product ideas into branded merchandise. Setting up a web store allows you to sell these products directly to your audience, turning your creative concepts into tangible goods they'll love.

When it comes to branding and packaging, the possibilities are virtually limitless. From clothing and accessories to novelty items and collectibles, there's no shortage of products you can create to cater to your audience's interests.

To get started, brainstorm ideas, conduct market research, and analyze the feasibility of your product concepts. Engage with your audience to gather feedback and gauge their interest in your merchandise ideas. By leveraging your unique brand and connection with your audience, you can build a successful merchandise business that complements your content creation efforts.

## 2. <u>Use YouTube Shopping</u>

Expand your reach and streamline the shopping experience for your audience by selling products directly through YouTube. With YouTube Shopping, you can seamlessly integrate links to your products into your videos and YouTube Shorts, providing viewers with convenient access to purchase your merchandise.

There are various ways to showcase and sell your products on YouTube:

**Official Store on Your Channel:** Set up an official store on your channel where viewers can browse and purchase your products directly.

**Product Shelf Below Your Content:** Display a product shelf below your videos, showcasing your merchandise and allowing viewers to make purchases while watching your content.

**Shopping Button Within Your Content:** Integrate a shopping button within your videos, enabling viewers to explore and purchase your products without leaving the video player.

Pinned Product During Live Streams: During YouTube Live streams, pin products to the chat or stream interface, making it easy for viewers to discover and purchase items in real-time.

Whether you choose to utilize YouTube's built-in shopping features or leverage external platforms like Etsy, selling merchandise directly through YouTube offers a convenient and engaging way to monetize your content and connect with your audience.

Linking your storefronts and integrating YouTube Shopping is an effective way to drive traffic to your merchandise and enhance your sales strategy. To be eligible for YouTube Shopping, you must meet the following criteria:

**Join the YouTube Partner Program**: To participate in YouTube Shopping, you need to be a member of the YouTube Partner Program or have an Official Artist Channel.

**Comply with Content Guidelines:** Ensure that your channel is not designated as 'Made for Kids' and does not predominantly feature content targeted at children. This ensures that your channel aligns with YouTube's content policies.

**Maintain Compliance with Community Guidelines:** Avoid receiving Hate Speech Community Guideline Strikes on your channel, as this may disqualify you from accessing YouTube Shopping features.

149

By meeting these requirements, you can leverage YouTube Shopping to seamlessly integrate your storefronts and offer viewers a convenient way to explore and purchase your merchandise directly from your channel.

### 3. <u>Use affiliate links</u>

Affiliate marketing offers creators a unique opportunity to earn revenue by promoting products through specialized hyperlinks. When viewers click on these links and make purchases, creators receive a commission. While affiliate marketing isn't a quick way to get rich, it provides a steady stream of passive income for creative individuals.

As for monetization through the YouTube Partner Program, having 500 subscribers is indeed a prerequisite. However, earning opportunities expand for channels with over 1,000 subscribers. While advertising and YouTube Premium are reserved for channels with higher subscriber counts, alternative options such as channel membership and third-party subscription platforms offer additional avenues for monetization.

In summary, while 500 subscribers are required to initiate monetization with the YouTube Partner Program, creators can explore various revenue streams, including affiliate marketing, to supplement their income and grow their channel's profitability over time.

## 4.  <u>Channel membership</u>

If you've cultivated a dedicated fan base, channel membership offers another avenue to monetize your YouTube channel. To access this feature, you must first be a member of the YouTube Partner Program.

Once you've unlocked channel membership, you can customize the perks and pricing for different tiers of membership. It's essential to set reasonable prices, as members are charged monthly. Offering perks such as one-on-one chats and discounts on merchandise can entice fans to sign up for membership.

However, it's important to note that YouTube takes a 30% cut of the monthly membership fee. Therefore, when setting membership prices and planning perks, it's crucial to strike a balance between providing value to your fans and ensuring sustainable earnings for yourself.

### 5.  Use a third-party subscription platform

Platforms like Patreon and Buy Me A Coffee offer creators a direct avenue to engage with fans outside of YouTube's confines. By providing exclusive content, early access to videos, polls to determine future content, and discounts on merchandise, creators can attract fans to these platforms and generate additional income.

Furthermore, leveraging social media platforms for paid brand sponsorships can expand your revenue streams. Many YouTubers maintain active profiles on various social media platforms, allowing them to reach new audiences and attract potential brand partnerships. Brands may be interested in collaborating on sponsored content across multiple channels, including YouTube and other social media platforms.

However, it's crucial to consider the metrics and analytics associated with these partnerships. Brands seek a return on investment, so creators must demonstrate a combination of audience reach and engagement to secure lucrative brand deals. By showcasing your influence and engagement across multiple platforms, you can enhance your attractiveness to potential brand partners and maximize your earning potential.

## 6. Use your expertise to do freelance work

As you hone your videography skills through running a successful YouTube channel, you also develop the ability to create compelling content, market it effectively, and attract an engaged audience.

With this expertise, opportunities to collaborate with businesses may arise naturally, or you can proactively pitch your services to them. You can offer freelance videography services or enter into partnerships with brands, leveraging your skills to create impactful content that aligns with their marketing objectives.

Having a portfolio of your work from your YouTube channel allows you to showcase your capabilities to potential clients or brands. Whether it's producing promotional videos, capturing events, or creating branded content, your experience as a YouTuber equips you with valuable skills that can translate into professional opportunities in the videography industry.

**Key points to remember for making money on YouTube**

**When it comes to making money on YouTube, it's essential to keep several key points in mind:**

**Persistence Pays Off:** Making money on YouTube is a long-term endeavor that requires consistent effort and dedication. While success may not happen overnight, staying committed to your channel can lead to significant rewards over time.

**Reapplying to the YouTube Partner Program:** If your channel is initially rejected from the YouTube Partner

Program, don't be discouraged. You can reapply after 30 days, giving you the opportunity to address any issues and improve your channel's eligibility.

**Revenue Sharing:** Understand the revenue sharing models on YouTube. For AdSense revenue, creators receive 55% of advertising profits, while Super features and channel subscriptions follow a 70/30 split, with creators receiving the larger share.

**Payment Threshold:** You must reach a minimum threshold of $100 in earnings before YouTube sends funds to your bank account. Additionally, it can take up to 60 days for payments to be processed and deposited.

By keeping these key points in mind and maintaining a focus on quality content creation and audience engagement, you can position yourself for success and potentially generate a sustainable income from your YouTube channel.

# CHAPTER 9: DEALING WITH CHALLENGES AND SETBACKS

## *HANDLING NEGATIVE COMMENTS AND FEEDBACK*

Handling negative comments and feedback is an inevitable aspect of being a content creator on YouTube. While it's natural to feel disheartened or defensive when faced with criticism, it's crucial to approach these situations with professionalism and resilience. One of the first steps in managing negative feedback is to maintain perspective and recognize that not every comment will be positive. Understanding that criticism can provide valuable insights for improvement can help you view negative feedback as an opportunity for growth rather than a personal attack.

When responding to negative comments, it's essential to remain calm and composed. Avoid reacting impulsively or engaging in heated arguments with viewers, as this can escalate the situation and reflect poorly on your channel. Instead, take a moment to assess the comment objectively and consider whether a response is necessary. In some cases, it may be best to ignore inflammatory or derogatory remarks altogether, as engaging with trolls can often be counterproductive.

However, constructive criticism should be acknowledged and addressed respectfully. If a viewer raises valid concerns or points out areas for improvement, consider thanking them for their feedback and explaining any steps you plan to take in response. Demonstrating a willingness to listen to your audience and make changes based on their input can foster a sense of trust and loyalty among your viewers.

It's also important to establish boundaries and prioritize your mental well-being when dealing with negative comments.

Remember that you are not obligated to tolerate harassment or abuse from viewers, and it's perfectly acceptable to block or report individuals who engage in toxic behavior. Surround yourself with a supportive community of fellow creators and viewers who can offer encouragement and advice during challenging times.

Ultimately, handling negative comments and feedback is an ongoing process that requires patience, resilience, and a commitment to professionalism. By maintaining perspective, responding thoughtfully, and prioritizing your well-being, you can navigate criticism effectively and continue to cultivate a positive and supportive environment on your YouTube channel.

# *OVERCOMING PLATEAUS IN CHANNEL GROWTH*

As a content creator on YouTube, encountering plateaus in channel growth is a common challenge that many creators face. These plateaus can be frustrating and demotivating, but they also present opportunities for reflection, adaptation, and strategic planning to reignite momentum and propel your channel forward. To overcome plateaus in channel growth, it's essential to adopt a proactive and strategic approach.

One effective strategy for overcoming plateaus is to assess and analyze your content and channel performance thoroughly. Take a close look at your analytics to identify trends, patterns, and areas for improvement. Pay attention to metrics such as audience retention, click-through rate, and watch time to gain insights into viewer behavior and preferences. By understanding what content resonates most with your audience, you can tailor your future content strategy to better meet their needs and interests.

Experimentation and innovation are also key components of overcoming plateaus in channel growth. Don't be afraid to try new formats, topics, or styles of content to keep your audience engaged and attract new viewers. Embrace creativity and explore different ways to differentiate your channel from others in your niche. Whether it's collaborating with other creators, exploring trending topics, or incorporating interactive elements into your videos, innovation can help breathe new life into your channel and reignite audience interest.

Consistency is another crucial factor in overcoming plateaus in channel growth. Maintain a regular upload schedule and strive to deliver high-quality content consistently. Consistency not only helps to keep your audience engaged and coming back for more but also signals to the YouTube algorithm that your channel is active and relevant, potentially boosting your visibility and reach.

Building and nurturing a supportive community around your channel can also be instrumental in overcoming plateaus in growth. Engage with your audience through comments, live streams, and social media platforms to foster a sense of connection and belonging.

Encourage viewer interaction and feedback, and demonstrate appreciation for your audience's support and contributions. A loyal and engaged community can help amplify your channel's growth efforts through word-of-mouth promotion and sharing your content with others.

Finally, patience and persistence are essential virtues to cultivate when overcoming plateaus in channel growth. Rome wasn't built in a day, and neither is a successful YouTube channel. Stay focused on your long-term goals, remain adaptable to changes and challenges, and keep pushing forward, even in the face of setbacks.

With dedication, resilience, and strategic planning, you can overcome plateaus in channel growth and continue to thrive as a content creator on YouTube.

# *STAYING MOTIVATED AND PERSISTENT*

Staying motivated and persistent as a content creator on YouTube is essential for long-term success in a highly competitive and ever-evolving platform.

While it's natural to encounter challenges, setbacks, and moments of doubt along the way, maintaining a positive mindset and a resilient attitude can help you navigate obstacles and stay focused on your goals. Here are some strategies to help you stay motivated and persistent on your YouTube journey:

**Define Your Why:** Take some time to reflect on why you started your YouTube channel in the first place. What are your passions, interests, and long-term aspirations? Clarifying your purpose and vision can provide you with a sense of direction and motivation to keep pushing forward, even during challenging times.

**Set Clear Goals:** Establishing clear and achievable goals for your channel can help you stay focused and motivated.

Whether it's reaching a certain number of subscribers, increasing watch time, or improving video quality, setting specific, measurable, and realistic goals can provide you with milestones to work towards and celebrate along the way.

**Celebrate Progress:** Acknowledge and celebrate your achievements, no matter how small they may seem. Whether it's reaching a subscriber milestone, receiving positive feedback from viewers, or mastering a new editing technique, taking time to recognize your progress can boost your confidence and motivation to keep going.

**Embrace Challenges as Opportunities:** Instead of viewing challenges as roadblocks, see them as opportunities for growth and learning. Every setback or obstacle you encounter is a chance to refine your skills, experiment with new approaches, and ultimately become a better content creator.

**Find Inspiration:** Surround yourself with sources of inspiration and creativity that fuel your passion for content creation. Whether it's watching videos from your favorite creators, reading books on creativity and entrepreneurship, or attending industry events and conferences, exposing yourself to new ideas and perspectives can reignite your enthusiasm for your channel.

**Stay Organized and Consistent:** Establishing a structured workflow and maintaining consistency in your content creation process can help you stay on track and avoid feeling overwhelmed. Create a content calendar, set aside dedicated time for filming and editing, and prioritize tasks based on their importance and urgency.

**Take Breaks and Practice Self-Care:** Burnout is a real concern for content creators, so it's crucial to prioritize your mental and physical well-being. Take regular breaks, disconnect from your channel when needed, and engage in activities that recharge your batteries and reduce stress.

**Surround Yourself with Supportive People:** Build a network of fellow creators, friends, and mentors who understand the challenges of content creation and can offer encouragement, advice, and support when you need it most. Having a supportive community can make all the difference in staying motivated and persistent on your YouTube journey.

By implementing these strategies and staying committed to your passion for content creation, you can overcome obstacles, stay motivated, and ultimately achieve success on YouTube. Remember that success rarely happens overnight, so stay patient, stay persistent, and keep pushing forward towards your goals.

# CONCLUSION

In conclusion, embarking on a journey as a content creator on YouTube is a thrilling and rewarding endeavor, filled with endless possibilities for creativity, growth, and connection. Throughout this book, we've delved into the essential strategies, techniques, and insights to help you navigate the complexities of starting and growing a successful YouTube channel.

From defining your niche and creating compelling content to monetizing your channel and engaging with your audience, each chapter has provided valuable guidance and practical advice to empower you on your YouTube journey.

As you reflect on the insights shared in this book, remember that success on YouTube is not solely determined by numbers or metrics but by the impact you make on your audience and the fulfillment you derive from sharing your passion with the world. Embrace the journey, celebrate your progress, and remain committed to continuous learning and improvement as you navigate the ever-evolving landscape of content creation on YouTube.

Recapping the key points covered throughout this book, we've emphasized the importance of defining your niche and target audience, creating high-quality and engaging content, optimizing your channel for growth and monetization, and fostering meaningful connections with your audience.

By staying true to your unique voice and vision, staying consistent in your efforts, and staying resilient in the face of challenges, you can position yourself for success as a content creator on YouTube.

For new YouTubers embarking on their journey, I encourage you to embrace curiosity, creativity, and experimentation. Don't be afraid to take risks, try new things, and learn from both successes and failures. Stay patient and persistent, knowing that growth takes time, and success is often the result of perseverance and dedication.

As you continue to build and grow your channel, consider the next steps for expanding your reach and impact. Explore opportunities for collaboration with other creators, diversify your revenue streams through monetization features like channel memberships and merchandise, and stay informed about emerging trends and best practices in content creation and digital marketing.

Above all, remember that your journey as a content creator on YouTube is uniquely yours. Stay true to yourself, stay passionate about your content, and stay committed to making a positive impact on your audience and community. With dedication, resilience, and a willingness to learn and adapt, you have the power to create something truly special and meaningful on YouTube. Embrace the possibilities, seize the opportunities, and let your creativity shine as you embark on this exciting adventure.